# THERE GOES THE NEIGHBORHOOD

## Ten Buildings People Loved to Hate

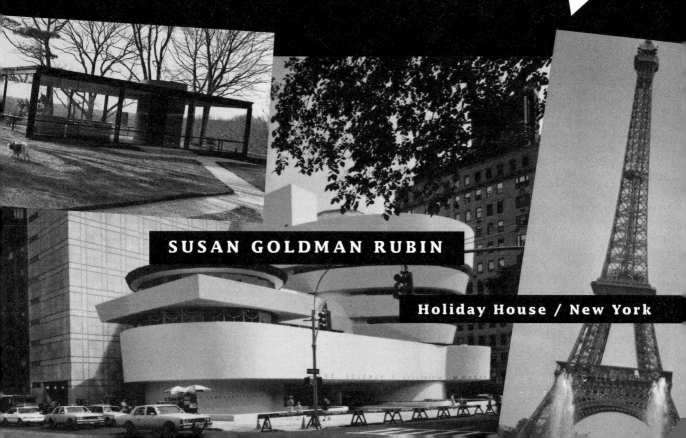

SUSAN GOLDMAN RUBIN

Holiday House / New York

*To my neighbors, the Gilsons—Bud, Sandy, Andy, and Liz*

## ACKNOWLEDGMENTS

Many people helped me with this book. I want to thank Philip Johnson and his assistant at the Glass House, Marty Skrelunas; Marilyn O'Rourke and Sharon Turo at the New Canaan Historical Society; Frank O. Gehry and Associates—especially Frank and Berta Gehry and Mr. Gehry's assistant, Keith Mendenhall; Jonathan Drezner, architect; Mary Ann Campbell and Gary Cooper at the Walker Community Library; architect Alan Hess; Ilene Magaras at the Guggenheim Museum archives; John Lockwood, historian at the Washington Monument; Paul Goldberger; and Mike Noble. Special thanks to my husband, Michael, and our son Andy. And finally, a bouquet of thank-yous to my agent, George Nicholson, and my editor, Mary Cash, for their good humor and love of art.

## ILLUSTRATIONS CREDITS

Courtesy of the Réunion des Musées Nationaux / Art Resource, NY: 4 (upper photos), 14 (lower), 16, 17, 18, 20 • Courtesy of the McDonald's Corporation, © Ray Reiss: 4 (lower photos) • Courtesy of Michael B. Rubin, © Michael B. Rubin: 6 (right), 64 (refrigerator) • Courtesy of the Library of Congress: 6 (left), 8, 10, 12, 22, 26 • Courtesy of Richard Hewett, © Richard Hewett: 14 (top) • Courtesy of the Warshaw Collection, Archives Center, National Museum of American History, Smithsonian Institution: 22 (photo of iron) • Courtesy of The New-York Historical Society, © Collection of The New-York Historical Society: 24, 28 • Courtesy of Richard Payne, © Richard Payne, FAIA: 25, 30 • Courtesy of the collection of Leah Schall: 27 • Courtesy of the New Canaan Historical Society, Susan Behr, Photographer: 31 • Courtesy of Philip Johnson, © Philip Johnson: 32, 35, 37 • Courtesy of Frank O. Gehry, © Frank O. Gehry: 38 (photos of house exterior), 41 • Courtesy of Tim Street Porter/Esto, © Tim Street Porter/Esto. All rights reserved.: 38 (photos of house interior), 42 • Courtesy of Michael Webb, © Michael Webb: 43, 44, 80 (bottom), 83 • Courtesy of AKG London: 46, 49, 50, 51 • Courtesy of Disney Enterprises, Inc., © Disney Enterprises, Inc.: 53 • Courtesy of Gwathmey Siegel & Associates Architects: 54 (museum exterior) • Courtesy of the Archives Center, National Museum of American History, Smithsonian Institution: 54 (toilet) • Courtesy of SRGF, © SRGF, NY, Photograph by David Heald: 54 (museum interior), 62 • Courtesy of the Solomon R. Guggenheim Museum, Ben Greenhaus, photographer: 57 • Courtesy of The Cartoon Bank, © the New Yorker Collection 1958 Allen Dunn from cartoonbank.com. All Rights Reserved: 60 • Courtesy of the Frank Lloyd Wright Archives: 61 • Courtesy of The Cartoon Bank, © the New Yorker Collection 1976 James Stevenson from cartoonbank.com. All Rights Reserved: 63 • Courtesy of Renzo Piano Building Workshop, © M. Denance: 64 (building exterior) • Courtesy of Renzo Piano Building Workshop, © Renzo Piano and Richard Rogers: 64 (sketches), 66 • Courtesy of Renzo Piano Building Workshop: 69, 71 • Courtesy of The Leonard Parker Associates, © The Leonard Parker Associates: 72 (center), 51 • Courtesy of The Leonard Parker Associates, © The Leonard Parker Associates, Balthazar Korab • photographer: 72 (top and bottom), 77 • Courtesy of The Leonard Parker Associates, © The Leonard Parker Associates, George Heinrich, photographer: 78 • Courtesy of the McDonald's Corporation, © Ray Reiss: 80 (top three photos), 86.

Library of Congress Cataloging-in-Publication Data
Rubin, Susan Goldman.
    There goes the neighborhood : 10 buildings people loved to hate / by Susan Goldman Rubin.
      p.   cm.
    Includes bibliographical references and index.
    ISBN 0-8234-1435-3 (hardcover)
    1. Architecture—Public opinion—Juvenile literature.   2. Architecture—United States—Juvenile literature.   3. Architecture—Europe—Juvenile literature.
    [1. Architecture.]   I. Title.
NA2599.5 .R83 2001
   720—dc21
                                                00-036953

# Contents

# Introduction

WHAT DO THE EIFFEL TOWER and McDonald's have in common?

One is a graceful iron tower, a wonder of engineering, the symbol of France. The other is a showy fast-food restaurant, one of the best-known images in America and throughout the world.

Believe it or not, when both structures were being built they made people in their neighborhoods furious before they were even finished. When Parisians first saw plans for the Eiffel Tower, they signed a petition and begged the city not to ruin their neighborhood by building it.

McDonald's restaurants have caused uproars in New York City, France, and elsewhere. Grown people have dumped rotten fruit in McDonald's parking lots. They didn't want a fast-food restaurant with "Golden Arches" spoiling *their* neighborhood.

There are all kinds of buildings that people hated at first. People have detested buildings so much they have thrown rocks at the windows, fired guns at them, and sued to stop their construction. There goes the neighborhood! they thought. Yet, eventually, many of these buildings became popular and even won prizes because they were beautiful, useful, or wildly original. How did these architectural eyesores become icons—beloved symbols of cities, countries, and cultures?

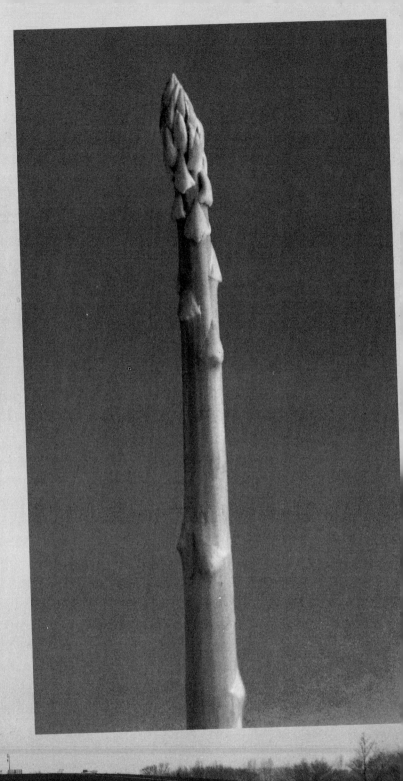

"A **DISGRACE** TO OUR PEOPLE."

"IT LOOKS LIKE A STALK OF **ASPARAGUS**."

# CHAPTER ONE

# The Washington Monument, Washington, D.C.

THE WASHINGTON MONUMENT has been described as "an exclamation point five hundred and fifty-five feet high." Actually the monument measures 555 feet and 5 $\frac{1}{8}$ inches. It is such a familiar landmark that people refer to it simply as "the monument." Yet it almost wasn't built.

The controversy surrounding the monument began in August 1783 when Congress unanimously agreed to erect a monument honoring George Washington. Congress wanted to put up a bronze statue of Washington on horseback. Pierre-Charles L'Enfant, a Frenchman chosen by Washington to design the new capital city, picked the exact spot for the statue. It would be on a wide, grassy park called the Mall that would stretch down to the future Capitol. Although Washington was flattered, he didn't want a monument to be built while he was still alive. And later, when he became president, he felt that a $5,000 statue would be a waste of money when the country needed more important things.

After Washington died in 1799, Congress voted again to build a monument honoring him. This time, instead of a statue, they planned a mausoleum, or grand tomb, made of granite and shaped like a pyramid. But the War of 1812 broke out and interrupted plans. By the time the war ended, the country didn't have enough money to begin building. So a group of citizens organized the Washington National Monument Society in 1833 to raise money for

A sketch of the winning design for the Washington Monument by Robert Mills, 1836

the project. The society asked everyone, even school children, to send in contributions. By 1836, they had raised about $28,000. The society held a competition for a new design, and many artists submitted sketches. The winner was Robert Mills, an architect and engineer from Charleston, South Carolina.

Mills's design included a 600-foot-high obelisk rising from a circular Greek temple with columns. Behind the columns he planned to put statues of important Americans. And at the top of the obelisk, there would be a "lookout gallery." The cost? A million dollars. Of course, the society loved Mills's design, but critics called it a hodgepodge "of Greek, Babylonian, and Egyptian architecture." Some members of Congress even disapproved of the site.

Nonetheless, on July 4, 1848, the cornerstone was laid and construction began. Since there wasn't enough money for the Greek temple and fancy statues, the society decided to build only the obelisk, but people objected. Some compared the obelisk to a stalk of asparagus. An editorial in the *New York Tribune* called it "a wretched design, a wretched location," and described it as "the big furnace chimney on the Potomac Flats." A bill prohibiting the monument was introduced in the Senate and caused heated debates.

But building continued anyway. Individuals, states, even foreign countries contributed blocks of stone inscribed with their names for the inside walls. One block was donated by the Franklin Fire Company of Washington, D.C. Another came from "Ladies & Gentlemen of the Dramatic Profession of America." Greece sent a piece of white marble from the ruins of the Parthenon, their ancient temple in Athens.

By 1854, the monument reached a height of 152 feet. Many feared that if it ever was built to full height, it might fall over. But there wasn't enough money and materials to finish the project anyway. Mills died in 1855. When the Civil War began in 1861, all work on the monument stopped.

During the war, the Union army used the Mall to drill soldiers. They set up a stockyard and slaughterhouse to feed the troops.

Cows grazed beneath the unfinished monument. A cartoon in *Frank Leslie's Illustrated Newspaper* of 1862 showed the scene with the caption: "Beef Depot Monument." Garbage piled up.

A cartoon from *Frank Leslie's Illustrated Newspaper,* 1862

Mark Twain, who worked as a Washington newspaperman in 1867, described the "memorial chimney" with "cow-sheds about its base, and the contented sheep nibbling pebbles . . . that surround it, and the tired pigs dozing in the holy calm of its protecting shadow." Twain predicted that by the time the monument got finished, Washington wouldn't be the "Father of our Country," he'd be the "Great-Great-Great-Grandfather!" After the war the unfinished monument stood there like a stump. The *New York Herald* called it "a disgrace to our people."

As the one hundredth anniversary of America's independence approached, interest in finishing the monument revived. Congress appointed a committee that decided a simple stone shaft would still be the best design. An engineer tested the foundation and thought it could only hold a monument 400 feet high. Many people felt that that would be a fine height for an obelisk. But others said that an obelisk was "inappropriate" and "heathenish." If completed it would look like "a tall and awkward smokestack." Some wanted to tear down the unfinished obelisk and start all over again.

Finally, in 1876, Congress passed a law to complete the monument once and for all. They appointed Lieutenant Colonel Thomas Lincoln Casey, an engineer, to take charge. But people argued about the design once again. Some thought they should complete the original obelisk designed by Mills. But Henry van Brunt, a leading architectural critic, said, "No person interested in our reputation as a civilized people can contemplate this completion without pain." Van Brunt suggested inviting architects to submit new designs. Ideas poured in for everything ranging from a Hindu pagoda to an English Gothic tower topped by an angel. Casey insisted on sticking with the original plan and building a simple obelisk, 550 feet high.

In October 1878 construction resumed. Casey discovered that the original foundation was actually too weak to support the weight of the stone shaft. So he strengthened the foundation and added supports made out of concrete. He used marble for the outside of the monument and granite as backing. From 450 feet up, though, the walls would be only marble. A crane lifted heavy pieces of marble through the interior to the top of the building. Although rope netting hung outside the walls to catch any workmen, no one fell or was injured on the job. Since construction had stopped for thirty years, a slightly different shade of marble finished the monument. Work progressed quickly.

At last an aluminum capstone was ready to be placed on the "pyramidion," or pyramid-shaped point. Casey chose aluminum because it would protect the monument from lightning storms, and it would not tarnish. Later he added copper rods as lightning conductors. The aluminum tip, weighing just 100 ounces, was the largest piece of that material ever cast. Tiffany, the New York City jewelry store, displayed it before it was set on the monument.

That day, December 6, 1884, a cold gale wind blew at 60 miles an hour. Spectators down on the Mall held their breath as they looked up at officials standing on scaffolding near the top. But the

capstone slid into place, an American flag was unfurled, and cannons boomed a salute. Everyone applauded. In spite of what they had once thought about the monument, the public's jeers now turned into cheers.

On February 21, 1885, President Chester A. Arthur formally dedicated the monument. All together it had taken 102 years to build! The monument didn't officially open to the public until 1888, when Casey installed an elevator and added a handrail for the stairs. Tourists took the twelve-minute ride up to the

An etching of the monument's elevator from *A Souvenir of the Federal Capital* by Hutchins and Moore, 1887 observation room in a "steam hoist," an elevator run by a steam-driven engine. Some people preferred climbing the 897 steps with a guide.

But critics kept complaining. A reviewer in the *American Architect and Building News* said: "It is . . . to be regretted that ages are likely to elapse before the monument will fall down."

However, Frederick Law Olmsted, Jr., a landscape architect, praised the Washington Monument in 1902 as "one of the most beautiful of human creations. Indeed, it is at once so great and so simple that it seems to be almost a work of nature." At the turn of the century, Olmsted worked on a committee to redesign the Mall and make the monument grounds more attractive. The committee planned not only to enlarge and beautify the Mall and line it with museums, but also to add a reflecting pool leading down to a new structure, the Lincoln Memorial. The Reflecting Pool was completed in December 1922.

Meanwhile, other improvements made the monument more appealing to visitors. In 1901 an electric elevator replaced the hoist lift, and today's elevator whisks people to the top in just one minute. However, some people still prefer the stairs. Several pranksters have tried to walk up on their hands. And one sixty-five-year-old man from Kentucky made five round trips while a newspaper reporter kept score.

In late 1997, the monument was closed for cleaning, repairs, and renovations. Finally, on July 31, 2000, it reopened to visitors. Then it closed again briefly while a new elevator was installed. The elevator has opaque walls that become transparent so passengers can see the commemorative stones *inside* the monument.

Over two million people come to see the monument every year. It is the tallest masonry structure in the world—that is, the stones are held together by their own weight without any metal reinforcement. Once called a stalk of asparagus, the monument is now considered "a simple, sublime shaft . . . rising nearer to the skies than any known monument on earth"—worthy of the man it honors.

"WE PROTEST WITH ALL OUR STRENGTH ... THE USELESS AND MONSTROUS EIFFEL TOWER"

CHAPTER TWO

# The Eiffel Tower,

## Paris, France

WHEN THE FRENCH GOVERNMENT announced plans for building the Eiffel Tower on the Champ de Mars, a residential neighborhood in Paris, people strongly objected. Forty-seven artists, writers, poets, composers, and cultural leaders, including Charles Garnier, the architect who had designed the Paris Opera House; Guy de Maupassant, author of short stories; and Alexandre Dumas, son of the novelist who wrote *The Three Musketeers,* sent an angry letter to the minister of public works. The letter said: "We protest with all our strength . . . the useless and monstrous Eiffel Tower. The Eiffel Tower . . . is without a doubt the dishonor of Paris. Everyone feels it, everyone says it, everyone is profoundly saddened by it."

At the end of the letter they predicted that Paris would become "the Paris of Monsieur Eiffel," and they were right!

Despite their protest, work on the tower went ahead. The French government planned an exposition for 1889 to celebrate the one hundredth anniversary of the French Revolution and the country's progress as an industrial power. The government wanted to create something spectacular that would draw visitors to the Paris Exposition and decided on a tower 1,000 feet high. At that time the tallest structure in the world was the Washington Monument, 555 feet and 5 $\frac{1}{8}$ inches high, but the French wanted to outdo the Americans. In May 1886, they held a competition and invited architects and engineers to submit designs. Over one hundred drawings came in, including one for a tower in the form of a gigantic water sprinkler to water Paris, and another for a huge guillotine to symbolize the French Revolution. Two engineers even suggested a stone tower topped with a powerful electric light bright enough to enable Parisians all over the city to read their newspapers.

But the judges unanimously chose an entry designed by engineer Gustave Eiffel. Eiffel proposed building a simple, graceful tower made of cast iron and anchored by four piers, or legs, curving inward. The tower would serve no purpose other than to attract worldwide attention.

A sketch of Gustave Eiffel's, 1886

Eiffel was a careful planner. He had thirty years' experience in building iron railroad bridges spanning rivers in France, Portugal, and Indochina. Most are still standing today.

Eiffel wanted to work with iron because it had strength as well as flexibility. Although steel was lighter and had more give, it could cause the tower to sway in high winds. Eiffel studied the effects of wind and made mathematical calculations. Before starting construction, he and his draftsmen turned out more than five thousand blueprints for every single piece of metal they planned to use. Eiffel understood that if he left open spaces in the iron structure, the wind would blow *through* the tower and not knock it over. In an interview with the newspaper *Le Temps,* he said: "What was the main obstacle I had to overcome in designing the tower? Its resistance to wind."

Eiffel offered to dismantle his iron tower if the City of Paris decided not to keep it. The city signed a contract with him on

January 8, 1887, and on January 26 Eiffel's crew began digging the foundation. People in the neighborhood immediately complained.

Although Champ de Mars had been the site of the Paris world's fairs in previous years, it was also a quiet family neighborhood near the Seine River. Tree-lined streets held lovely private houses and apartment buildings. When the neighbors saw the Eiffel Tower going up, they panicked. They thought that the "metal monster" would surely fall on their homes and crush them. One math professor figured out that if the tower ever reached the height of 748 feet it would definitely collapse. Neighbors also feared that as the tower went up it would affect the weather. In those days people didn't understand lightning very well. They thought that burying conduits from the tower's lightning rods in the bed of the Seine would kill the fish. People also worried that the tower would sink in the sandy clay soil of Champ de Mars. Headlines in *Le Matin,* a popular Paris newspaper, read: "THE TOWER IS SINKING."

Finally, one of the nervous neighbors brought a lawsuit against

**The first platform completed, March 1888**

the City of Paris to stop construction. Work came to a halt. The city didn't want to take responsibility for any damage to citizens or their homes. So Eiffel agreed to insure the neighbors himself. Now construction continued and the Eiffel Tower quickly rose.

Two hundred and fifty men worked on the job every day of the year. They hurried to complete the tower in time for the opening of the Paris Exposition scheduled for May 1889. By March 1888, they completed the first platform. By July they reached the second platform. Eiffel built a canteen for the workers on the first platform, then later on the second. They could eat their meals without wasting precious time by leaving the job site.

Under Eiffel's direction, teams of riveters bolted the metal pieces in place right on the tower. The beams, trusses, and girders had prepunched holes, like pieces of an Erector set. All the holes had to line up exactly, because of Eiffel's meticulous planning. Before he started building he knew precisely how much the tower would weigh—800 tons.

Parisians gathered to watch, both in awe and in horror. They thought the tower looked like "a hulking metal beast crouched on

**Under construction: December 20, 1888; January 20,1889; February 12, 1889; March 12, 1889**

all fours." Some called it an "elephant," others a "giraffe."

As the tower grew higher during the winter of 1889, workers suffered from the icy winds. Eiffel constructed wooden platforms around the high columns so that the men wouldn't have to look straight down and get dizzy. The only person who ever fell and was killed was a workman showing off for his girlfriend.

From the second platform up, the four separate piers converged to become one single column. By February the tower was almost finished. Curious visitors came and climbed up single file with Eiffel in the lead. There were 363 steps to the first platform and 381 to the second. Only the staff was allowed to climb the narrow spiral staircase of 927 steps leading to the very top.

Electrically powered elevators were a relatively new invention at that time. And the height to be reached in the Eiffel Tower was greater than any ever reached by an elevator. The curve of the piers created another difficulty. What kind of tracks would be needed? Eiffel refused to have elevators going straight up from the ground through the center space, because he thought it would spoil the beauty of his design. He hired three different companies to install separate systems. Leon Edoux, one of Eiffel's friends from school, created the elevator that carried tourists to the top. The whole trip from the ground level took only seven minutes!

Last of all, Eiffel put in souvenir stands and four restaurants, each offering a different kind of food. An observation deck on the third platform was enclosed in glass to protect sightseers from the wind. A spiral staircase coiled around the column from the third platform up to Eiffel's private apartment, which contained rooms he used for scientific experiments. Eiffel wanted his tower to serve useful purposes, so he created an observatory for studying weather. His instruments measured temperatures, rainfall, and wind speed.

By March 1889, the tower stood at its full height of 986 feet. It was the tallest structure in the world and remained so until 1929 when the Chrysler Building went up in New York City. Opening ceremonies took place on March 31, a rainy, windy day. Eiffel led the way to the top, raised the French flag, and made a speech thanking the engineers and workers. On May 6, 1889, the president of France officially opened the Paris Exposition and, naturally, the Eiffel Tower attracted most of the visitors. Crowds waited in line, as they still do today, for a chance to climb it, ride to the top, eat lunch or dinner there, and buy souvenirs. Souvenir stands throughout Paris sold miniatures of the Eiffel Tower, some small enough to be worn as charms on bracelets, others large enough to be made into reading lamps. There were tower-shaped wine bottles, bottle openers, salt and pepper shakers, candles, and models made of metal and paper. Pictures of the Eiffel Tower appeared on plates, music boxes, and postcards.

Millions of tourists came from all over France and other parts of the world. Kings, queens, dukes, duchesses, as well as ordinary people, thronged the tower and signed the guest book. Celebrity guests included Thomas Edison, who went up many times.

What did the French critics think now? Congratulations poured in, even from most of those forty-seven artists, writers, and composers who had sent that angry letter of protest. All except Guy de Maupassant. He complained that because of the tower the streets were jammed with tourists. "Not a single taxi is free," he said. "No driver will consent to drive you anywhere but to the Exposition.

GUSTAVE EIFFEL (1855)

Cartoon from the journal
*Le Central,* 1889

Besides, the only customers they want are the flashy foreigners."
Friends no longer gave dinner parties, he grumbled, or invited him
to eat anyplace except the Eiffel Tower. De Maupassant hated it so
much that he often ate lunch there in a restaurant on the second
platform. That was the only place in the city where he wouldn't
have to see "this tall skinny pyramid of iron ladders, this giant and
disgraceful skeleton."

After the Exposition closed in early November, the exhibition
halls and displays were torn down, but the Eiffel Tower remained
standing. Some critics still thought it was ugly and said it "stood up
from Paris like a hat pin." But others found it beautiful and
inspiring. Artists such as Georges Seurat, Pablo Picasso, Marc
Chagall, and Henri Rousseau painted the Eiffel Tower in their many
different styles. The changing views from the Eiffel Tower
fascinated Robert Delaunay so much that he painted it over and
over again from 1909 to 1911.

In 1909 the Eiffel Tower was almost torn down. Twenty years
had passed since Eiffel had built the tower, and according to his
contract, it now belonged to the City of Paris. Rumors spread that
the tower might be moved or even scrapped. It badly needed
expensive repairs. Just repainting the tower took 50 tons of rust-
free paint. The painting had to be done with brushes and rollers
because spray guns would spatter paint all over the neighborhood.

Around that time radio was becoming popular. A transmitter was
set up on top of the tower and served as a communications post
during World War I. After the war, news programs and then concerts
were broadcast from the tower. Later, in 1934, France's first
television transmitter went up on the tower, adding to its height
and giving it a grand total of 1,052 feet and 4 inches. So Eiffel's
goal, to make the tower useful, was fulfilled.

Today the monument receives twice as many visitors each year
as the Louvre Museum. Almost every brochure or travel book about
France shows an image of the Eiffel Tower. That "hat pin" sticking
up from Paris has become a symbol not only of the city, but also of
the whole country.

"WIND PLAYS **HAVOC** WITH WOMEN AT THE FLATIRON."

"**STRONG WINDS WILL SURELY BLOW IT OVER.**"

"TWENTY-THREE **SKIDDOO!**"

# CHAPTER THREE

# The Flatiron Building,

## New York, New York

WHEN THE TRIANGULAR FULLER Building went up in New York City in 1902, some people said that it looked like an iron, the kind used for pressing clothes. So they jokingly called it the Flatiron, and the nickname stuck. Others thought the wedge-shaped building resembled "a stingy piece of pie." And there were those who said it looked like an ocean liner sailing up Fifth Avenue.

The Flatiron shocked New Yorkers when it was completed. At twenty-three stories high it was the tallest building north of City Hall. A skyscraper. Although twenty-three stories may not seem so high today, in those days buildings taller than five or six stories alarmed people. How could they climb so many flights of stairs? How would they get enough light and fresh air? What if there were a fire—how would they get out?

Skyscrapers first appeared in Chicago after a terrible fire called "the Great Fire" swept through Chicago in October 1871 and destroyed thousands of buildings in the center of the city. One of the reasons that so many buildings caught fire was that they were made of wood. Even the buildings constructed with stone and brick had wood frames. So when architects and engineers began to rebuild they used a new material—steel.

Steel girders framed the buildings on the inside and formed a "skeleton." Outside walls were still made of stone and brick to

appear strong to those who doubted the safety of skyscrapers. Building tall seemed an efficient way to utilize space. And new developments like electric lights, elevators, indoor toilets, and telephones made it possible.

A leading architect who designed skyscrapers in Chicago during the 1880s and 1890s was Daniel Hudson Burnham. He and his partner, John Wellborn Root, figured out a way to anchor high-rise buildings in the soggy soil with concrete foundations. In 1882, Burnham and Root's ten-story Montauk Building in Chicago became the first fireproof office building. It may have been the first building to be called a "skyscraper," according to some art historians. But most authorities say that the Home Insurance Building by William Le Baron in 1885 was the first skyscraper.

Root died in 1891, but Burnham carried on. His Reliance Building in 1894 featured more glass than had ever been used before on the surface of an office building. Continuous bands of windows not only looked beautiful, but also let in fresh air and natural light.

As Burnham continued to create innovative structures, his reputation grew. To make sure that his buildings went up properly and efficiently, Burnham worked with George B. Fuller, a Chicago-based engineer and contractor.

One of the clients who came to Burnham and Fuller was Winfield A. Stratton, a Colorado gold miner who had struck it rich. Stratton asked them to design a luxurious house in Colorado. Instead, they talked him into building what would be the tallest office building in the country, and situating it in New York City. Stratton went along with the idea and a public announcement of the building came in November 1900. Although Fuller died that year, his son-in-law took over his company. The Fuller Company developed the Flatiron, became part owner, and gave the building its official name, the Fuller Building.

The site posed an interesting problem. It was an unusual

**The lower limestone levels and ornately decorated terra cotta upper levels**

V-shaped or triangular lot at the intersection of Broadway and Fifth Avenue at Twenty-third Street. The building took its shape from the lot, and filled it to the very edges.

Arched entrances on both Fifth Avenue and Broadway led into the building. Some critics complained because there wasn't one main entrance. The outer walls were made of limestone on the lower levels, and terra-cotta above. Ornate patterns of flowers, leaves, shells, and Grecian motifs decorated all the surfaces.

Every office contained windows looking out. Standing in an office on the sixteenth floor at the narrow end of the building, only 6 feet wide, is like gazing at the view from the prow of a ship. Straight ahead a person can see all the way uptown to Times Square and Forty-second Street. Through a window to the right is the East River, and to the left, the Hudson River.

The Fifth Avenue side faces Madison Square, a little park. In 1903 the neighborhood was considered one of the most stylish in New York. The blocks around the Flatiron formed the center of publishing, fashion, and retail businesses.

From the moment construction of the Flatiron began in 1901, it disrupted the neighborhood and aroused criticism. Since the Flatiron was twice as tall as other buildings in the area, it stood out. A journalist writing about it in the *Architectural Record* of May 1902 said Burnham's "building is at present quite the most notorious

**Under construction, 1902**

THE FLATIRON BUILDING. N.Y.
This is the place to raise the wind. — Yours.
Design only copyrighted by Chas. Rose 1908.

A popular postcard, 1908

thing in New York, and attracts more attention than all the other buildings now going up put together."

People predicted that strong winds would surely blow it over. According to historian Oliver Jensen, spectators stood around, at a safe distance, of course, waiting to watch it crumble, and bet that when it did, "the debris would scatter as far as Madison Avenue," one block away. However, the Fuller Construction Company published an advertisement claiming that their building was solid. "From a structural standpoint," it read, "it is the strongest building ever erected." The Flatiron was anchored in bedrock, an ideal foundation for a skyscraper.

But the height of the building combined with its unusual shape created a downdraft, or wind. "WIND PLAYS HAVOC WITH WOMEN AT THE FLATIRON," read a headline in the *New York Herald* of January 31, 1903. The article reported how "women were inconveniently blown about and paper money lost from their pocketbooks." Gusts of wind lifted the long skirts that women wore in those days and revealed their ankles, creating a spectacle. Men stood around and gawked. Policemen directing traffic chased the men away by shouting, "Twenty-three skiddoo!" which meant, go away from Twenty-third Street!

One day at the Flatiron a sudden blast of wind blew so hard that it pushed a messenger boy into Fifth Avenue, where he was killed by a passing automobile. Windstorms around the Flatiron often broke windows throughout the neighborhood. Tourists regarded

these "wild events" as "one of the peculiar features of Manhattan."

Yet the Flatiron quickly became a popular landmark. People flocked to see it. "The most striking of skyscrapers," commented a journalist. Images of the Flatiron appeared on postcards and souvenir penny banks.

The graceful beauty of the Flatiron and its remarkable shape inspired many photographers. Alfred Stieglitz and Edward Steichen took misty romantic pictures of the building at dusk, framed by the trees in Madison Square.

Stieglitz recalled, "I remember my father coming upon me as I was photographing in the middle of Fifth Avenue. 'Alfred,' he said, 'how can you be interested in that hideous building?' 'Why Pa,' I replied, 'it is not hideous but the new America.'"

Today the Flatiron still stands—New York's oldest and most beloved skyscraper, "a great ship sailing up the avenue." The New York City Landmarks Preservation Commission takes care of it along with other historic buildings, neighborhoods, and parks. They want to save the Flatiron so that future generations can enjoy it and get a glimpse of the past.

**A view from Madison Square (left)**

"SCANDALOUS, INDECENT, AND SHOCKING TO THE TOWN."  "THEY'RE LOUSING UP THE COUNTRYSIDE WITH BUILDINGS MOST ALARMING."

# CHAPTER FOUR

# Philip Johnson's Glass House,

## New Canaan, Connecticut

IN 1946, PHILIP JOHNSON, a modernist architect, bought five acres of wooded land in New Canaan, Connecticut. Over the next three years he built a house for himself that was made of glass.

Although the low rectangular house wasn't visible past the stone wall on the road, his neighbors angrily complained that it ruined the look of their town. New Canaan was known for colonial-style houses two and three stories high, covered in clapboard or shingles, and featuring wide front porches and shuttered windows. Some people voiced their protest by writing funny poems published in the *New Canaan Advertiser,* a local newspaper. One verse by "Edgar Guess Who?" was a spoof of a verse called "Home" by Edgar A. Guest.

It takes a heap of livin' in a place
    to make it home.
And I wish those guys like Johnson
    would take their plans and roam.
They're lousing up the countryside
    with buildings most alarming,
It isn't like New Canaan, where
    everything's been charming . . .
Maybe I'm old-fashioned or maybe
    I'm not keen
But when I take my monthly bath
    I'd rather not be seen.

The Hanford-Sillman House, a typical colonial New Canaan home

Johnson didn't mind the put-downs. "I rejoice in rejection," he said with a chuckle.

Johnson's Glass House project started when he followed his friend and colleague, Eliot Noyes, from New York City to New Canaan. Both men had received their degrees in architecture from Harvard. And they both worked at the Museum of Modern Art in New York where Johnson had founded the Department of Architecture and Design. After Noyes built a modern one-story house for his family in New Canaan, he suggested that Johnson and their teacher and friend, Marcel Breuer, move there, too.

Johnson picked his parcel of rolling land on Ponus Ridge Road because it sloped down to a pond and halfway down, a little rocky shelf stuck out. "I chose the site because of the famous Japanese idea," he said. "Always put your house on a shelf, because the good

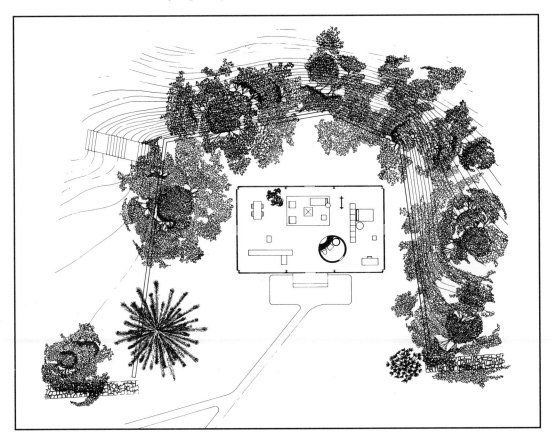

**The site plan of the Glass House**

spirits will be caught by the hill that's behind the house; the evil spirits will be unable to climb the hill below the house."

Johnson explained that he wanted to be connected with nature: "My house is a house in the field. That comes from my upbringing in Ohio. I love fields, pastures." As a landscape architect, he wished to combine art and nature. He made the house transparent so that he could look out at the old stone walls dating back to the eighteenth and nineteenth centuries, the meadows full of tall grasses and wildflowers, and, of course, the trees. "Trees are the basic building material of the place," he said. In designing his house he imitated the work of Ludwig Mies van der Rohe, a modern architect he greatly admired. "Mies had mentioned to me as early as 1945 how easy it would be to build a house entirely of large sheets of glass," Johnson recalled. Mies designed a similar rectangular glass house for Dr. Edith Farnsworth in Plano, Illinois, and showed Johnson the sketches.

It took Johnson three years to build his house. The house is made of glass from floor to ceiling and is held together by steel piers at the corners. The dining and living room areas are marked off simply by the arrangement of furniture, all designed by Mies, and a few pieces of art. Low cabinets separate the bedroom area

from the living room area. "From one side of the house you see the moon rise," said Johnson, "while from the other side you see the sun, both at the same time." There are no curtains or draperies except for a cluster of moveable

The living room area with furniture designed by Mies van der Rohe shades. "My house has beautiful wallpaper," said Johnson, referring to the birch trees, swamp maple, and white pine in the distance.

The house is anchored by a brick podium or platform and by a brick cylinder that goes through the flat roof. The cylinder contains a toilet, sink, and shower inside, and a fireplace on the outside. Backing up to a roaring fire in the winter was Johnson's idea of what a New England house should be. "The Glass House is a permanent camping trip protected from weather," he said. His favorite season for the house was winter when it snowed. "Then the snow comes down at night and the building floats," he said. "If the snow comes down at an angle, then it's as if you're in an elevator going up that way."

Johnson regarded his house as a private weekend retreat. During construction he also built the Brick Guest House, directly opposite. The two houses complemented each other—one solid, the other transparent.

Of course, a glass house posed problems. Birds flew into the house through the four doors that stayed open during warm weather. Wild turkeys crashed into the glass walls.

Townspeople couldn't understand why Johnson would give up his privacy and be so exposed. The saying goes that people who live in glass houses shouldn't throw stones. Once some of the neighbors *did* throw stones at the Glass House. Johnson, in return, went around throwing stones at some of his neighbors' windows. The prank got him into serious trouble and he wound up having to pay for the damage.

Before construction was even completed in 1949, curious people came to see the Glass House. Every Sunday there were parking problems and traffic jams as journalists and museum people flocked from New York City to New Canaan to photograph and visit the Glass House. Special police patrols had to be called in. *The New York Times* reported that throngs of visitors looked upon Johnson's "ultra-modern residence" with "awe, wonder and indignation."

Johnson enjoyed the attention, but his neighbors did not. The Glass House became the subject of heated debates. Some people called it "the desecration of the New Canaan countryside." Art historian Nina Bremer wrote that the "Glass House then seemed

**The Glass House and the brick guest house**

scandalous, indecent, shocking to the town." A New Canaan poet
calling herself "A Modern Miss" wrote this verse:

Give me the Gothic, or even Rococo;
Mr. Johnson, I think you're just plain
    loco.
The vine covered cottage is one of
    my joys;
I can't sympathize with his friend,
    Mr. Noyes.
I'm modern, believe me, in all the
    new fads,
But these architects are the worst
    kind of cads.

The "cads" in the poem were Landis Gores and John Johansen,
colleagues of Johnson's from Harvard. They loved his Glass House
so much that they, too, moved to New Canaan, opened offices there,

and built stark, simple modern houses. Now the neighbors were more furious than ever. They nicknamed Johnson and his pals "the Harvard Five," and accused them of turning New Canaan into a "laboratory for the International Style of the Modern movement." An ongoing battle raged for years between "the Traditionalists" and "the Moderns."

Johnson and the Harvard Five met frequently to critique one another's work and discuss problems. Finally, they thought of a way to appease the local residents and win them over. They decided to open their houses for a tour once a year. More than two thousand tickets were sold for the first tour, and the proceeds benefited the community nursery school.

The New Canaan Modern-House tour was such a huge success that it became an annual event. One woman visiting the Glass House told Johnson that she would never want to live there. He replied, "Madam, I haven't invited you."

Over the years Johnson kept purchasing additional land adjoining his estate until he had more than 40 acres. In 1962, he enlarged the pond below the Glass House and built a pavilion on it. The pavilion, made of concrete, is like a little island.

Next came an underground painting gallery to hold his museum-quality collection. Johnson wanted it to look like a natural mound of earth, a part of the landscape, rather than a formal building. And he didn't need any windows because sunlight might damage the paintings. In 1970, he built a separate gallery for his sculptures. Part of it is above ground, and part is underneath.

A few years later he realized that he needed a place to work. In the Glass House there were too many distractions—"Squirrels! Birds!" So Johnson built a little white stucco studio lit only by a skylight and a window. Inside, bookshelves line the walls behind a table and three chairs. Johnson said, "I don't invite many visitors into this space . . . it is really a place for one man to concentrate."

In 1985, he erected an unusual tower made of concrete blocks, dedicated to his friend Lincoln Kirstein. And more recently, he constructed a chain-link "Ghost House" honoring another friend, architect Frank O. Gehry, who likes to use chain link as a building material.

The American Institute of Architects (AIA) awarded its gold medal to Johnson in 1978 for the Glass House itself. The award honored the original structure as "a classic work of architecture which is as extraordinary and beautiful today as it was when it was built."

Johnson has decided to open the Glass House to the public after his death. He has built an electrically powered gate and a visitors' pavilion. Not only are the structures functional, but they also look like pieces of sculpture.

Johnson offered to will his entire estate to the New Canaan Historical Society, but the society turned him down. It couldn't afford to maintain the estate as a public museum and architectural exhibit.

So next he offered it to the National Trust for Historic Preservation. The Trust accepted the Glass House. But parking created a whole new controversy, which has not yet been settled.

Johnson, now in his nineties, lives in the Glass House year-round, enjoying the change of seasons. Architectural historian Vincent Scully once described the Glass House as "the age-old

American house in the woods." In 1986, Scully said Johnson's "place now joins, as no one thirty years ago could ever have thought it would, not only Taliesin West [Frank Lloyd Wright's home] but Monticello, too [Thomas Jefferson's home] as a major memorial to the complicated love affair Americans have with their land."

The Ghost House, Philip Johnson's homage to Frank O. Gehry

"IT'S A DIRTY THING TO DO IN SOMEBODY ELSE'S FRONT YARD."

"IF IT WOULD EVER LOOK COMPLETED, I MIGHT GET USED TO IT."

# CHAPTER FIVE

# Frank O. Gehry's House,

## Santa Monica, California

ARCHITECT FRANK O. GEHRY faced a challenge when his wife, Berta, found a house for them to live in. It was an old two-story pink bungalow in a quiet residential neighborhood in Santa Monica, California. But the house was too small for Gehry, Berta, their son, Alejandro, and another baby they hoped to have. And besides, Gehry wanted to experiment. "It was just a dumb little house with charm," he said, "and I became interested in trying to make it more important. I became fascinated with creating a shell around it." So Gehry added more room by wrapping a wild new house around the old one.

Construction began in January 1978. Using ordinary, inexpensive materials such as corrugated metal, chain-link fencing, and unfinished plywood, he surrounded the pink bungalow with walls shaped like abstract sculptures. Windows tilted at odd angles and offered views of the old house. No two sections looked alike. "I'm trying to do something different," he said.

"The house is different all right," wrote a journalist in the *Evening Outlook,* a local newspaper, in the summer of 1978 before construction was completed.

"The architect knew it would be offensive to people around," said a man who lived a few houses away from Gehry's. "It's a dirty thing to do in somebody else's front yard. If he were a poet, he'd be writing smutty jingles."

**Frank O. Gehry's House (left)**

John Dreyfuss, another journalist who lived nearby on Twenty-first Street, reported that "the neighbors are offended, baffled, amazed and angry at what Gehry has done. Many people think the house is in the wrong place."

But Gehry thought that the house was in exactly the *right* place on the corner of Washington Avenue and Twenty-second Street. It was a middle-class neighborhood like the ones he had lived in growing up in Canada, and later in the United States. The area featured a mix of modest old bungalows, Spanish-style houses, and small apartment buildings. There were campers and boats parked in driveways and lots of chain-link and concrete-block fencing. Gehry used these same industrial materials but in an original way.

His weird design, a blend of art and architecture, immediately attracted attention. When one of Gehry's outraged neighbors called Donna Swink, mayor of Santa Monica, to see if the house met legal building codes, the answer was yes. Gehry followed up by inviting the mayor to tour his house. "Once Frank explained what he was doing," said Mayor Swink, "I could see his vision. It was exciting. I think the house is a masterpiece. I love it."

Will Thorne wrote an article in the *Evening Outlook* and quoted Gehry. "What I'm trying to do," Gehry said, "is explore ways of using corrugated metal and create a work of art at the same time." Since he and Berta had a limited budget, he needed to build the house inexpensively. "Today people cannot afford to build the way they used to," he said, "and I think it behooves the architect to find new ways to help teach people."

The design began with sketches on a yellow legal pad. Gehry loves to doodle with pen and black ink, and always carries something to sketch with in his briefcase. Then his scribbles are developed into careful plans. Gehry's assistant, Paul Lubowicki, made many precise working drawings of the house based on thousands of Gehry's sketches. Together they built models of the whole structure and of details such as windows in Gehry's Santa Monica office/workshop. But the finished house closely resembles Gehry's first scribbled drawings.

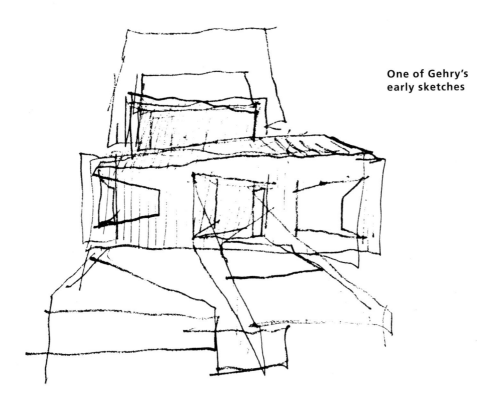

**One of Gehry's early sketches**

You enter on Twenty-second Street by opening a chain-link gate, the kind found in a school yard. Steps lead up to a door that opens up to another door, the one belonging to the old house. Inside, Gehry enlarged the living room by knocking down walls and stripping away plaster. He raised the ceiling and exposed beams and rafters but kept the original fireplace. The living room furniture includes chairs designed by Gehry that are made of corrugated cardboard. Natural light pours in everywhere through glass walls, windows, and skylights. All the windows are placed above eye level so that a person sitting inside the house can't see cars and pedestrians outside. One visitor said, "All you can see from the house are trees and sky."

Gehry kept a bay window in the living room wall to frame a view of the new kitchen and dining area. This contiguous space is a couple of steps below the old house. Here the floor is paved with black asphalt, the material used for roads and parking lots. There's even a drain so that the floor can be hosed down after a meal. Once when architect Philip Johnson came to dinner he joked, "Am I in the dining room or the driveway?"

The dining room furniture consists of a plain picnic table and bentwood chairs designed by Gehry and named for moves in ice hockey, his favorite sport. Over the table hangs a bare lightbulb dangling from a metal conduit. Above that, an asymmetrical corner skylight looks up into the branches of the trees outside. An

The dining room and kitchen

enormous kitchen window over the sink and stove is formed like a tilted cube.

Upstairs, more skylights and glass doors open to the trees. "The bedroom is like a tree house," said Gehry. "Lying in bed, looking toward the cedars, beams of sunlight stream in from behind and light up the beams and the chain-link creating a marvelous warmth."

Outside the master bedroom and Alejandro's room there's a deck enclosed by metal cyclone fencing. The metal fencing not only protected Alejandro from falling off, but it resembled a backstop on a baseball field and reminded Gehry of his childhood.

Down below, the yard was at first filled with sand. It served as a giant sandbox for Alejandro, and a couple of years later, his baby brother, Sam. The yard contained a spectacular desert cactus called euphorbia that was as tall as the old pink house. Gehry thought the cactus was so beautiful he wanted to share it with his neighbors, like a public sculpture. So he cut a trapezoid-shaped opening in one of the outer metal walls to provide a view of the plant to people passing by.

The house, even when completed, retained an unfinished look. This was exactly what Gehry intended. He left plywood walls and wooden joists bare and unpainted. "Buildings under construction look nicer than buildings finished," he said.

Gehry's fascination with raw materials and hardware stemmed from his childhood. As a young boy in Toronto, Canada, he played with bits and scraps from his grandfather's hardware store. His grandmother helped him build futuristic cities.

After Gehry and his family moved in, he was in shock for the first week. "It was

**Gehry at home**

like living in your own painting," he said. But soon the house became warm, friendly, and comfortable.

What did the neighbors think? One woman still disliked the unfinished appearance and was quoted in the *Evening Outlook.* "If it would ever look completed," she said, "I might get used to it." Some thought the chain-link fence made it look like a prison.

Another neighbor hated it so much that he fired a shot through the living room window, and the bullet is still lodged in the wall. But as Gehry's house drew national and international attention, most of the neighbors began to accept it. Some of them were even proud of it and brought their friends to see it.

Architects and critics published their comments.

"It is the most thought-provoking house in America, an amazing

A garden, added in 1987

collection of bits and pieces," said Philip Johnson. "It is my house thirty years later."

"The more you get to know it the more 'right' everything feels," said Tim Street-Porter. "It is then that you also realize that it really is a very cozy home, and never intimidating."

But Robert Campbell, a journalist for the *Boston Globe,* agreed with Gehry's hostile neighbors and wrote: "I probably wouldn't want him on my block either."

Despite the mixed reviews, the house won awards from the Southern California Chapter of the American Institute of Architects (AIA) in 1979, and from the national AIA in 1980.

By 1987, Gehry began plans for expanding the house to fit the changing needs of his family. But because of the demands of his busy architectural practice, remodeling didn't start until 1992. Gehry added a narrow exercise pool for swimming laps in the backyard and converted a small garage near the pool into a playroom for his children. A garden planted with succulents, bamboo, and prickly cactus softened the shocking appearance of the house and gave the Gehrys privacy. Students often drove by and sometimes knocked at the front door, hoping for a tour.

Critic Paul Goldberger wrote in *The New York Times* that "the Gehry house is a major work of architecture." Gehry successfully demonstrated that "it is possible to make comfort and beauty out of ugliness and ordinariness."

# CHAPTER SIX

# Neuschwanstein,

## Hohenschwangau, Germany;

# Sleeping Beauty

# Castle, Anaheim, California

"A MAN'S HOUSE is his castle," wrote Sir Edward Coke in the early seventeenth century. "Mad" King Ludwig II of Bavaria took these words literally when he built a castle for himself in the nineteenth century. During medieval times, most kings built castles not just for their own use but for hundreds of people—their families, soldiers, and servants—as a form of protection from their enemies. But not King Ludwig. His was a castle for one, a dream house. And it came to be called Neuschwanstein (pronounced Nush-von-stine), which means "new swan stone" in German. Swans were his favorite bird and he was known as the Swan King.

As a boy he loved spending time by himself, daydreaming and building with blocks. During the summers at Hohenschwangau, the royal family's castle in the Bavarian Highlands, he gazed at the view that would become the site of Neuschwanstein.

In 1864, when Ludwig was eighteen, his father, King Maximillian, died and Ludwig became king. At first the people liked him because they thought he looked so charming. Ludwig spent hours fussing over his appearance. "If I didn't have my hair curled every day," he said, "I couldn't enjoy my food." Government business didn't interest him, though.

King Ludwig II built Neuschwanstein in an inconvenient and inaccessible location on the ruins of an older castle, perched high on a crag in the Alps, 6,000 feet up. Not only did he love the spectacular view of the Pollat waterfall, he also liked being hard to reach. The king's ministers climbed the mountains with great difficulty if they needed to discuss important matters of state and present documents for him to sign. But King Ludwig II didn't care. He preferred theater and opera to running his country.

Heroes and heroines from medieval German poems captured his imagination. As a teenager he was so deeply moved by Richard Wagner's operas that he arranged to meet him, and they became close friends. Wagner's operas such as *Lohengrin, Parsifal,* and *Tristan and Isolde* inspired the castle. At that time in western Europe no one was building castles anymore. No one, that is, except "Mad" King Ludwig II. King Ludwig II dreamed up the design himself, modeling it after a medieval German knight's castle. Theater designer Christian Jank drew the sketches, which is perhaps why the castle looks more like a stage set than a residence. Architect Eduard Riedel carried out the plans, and construction began in 1869.

The building process began with blasting away part of the rocky hill to form a platform for the castle. Neuschwanstein was made of white limestone, the very stone at its base. Like other castles, it had spiky turrets, larger rounded towers, spires, and weather vanes. Inside, rooms were ornately decorated in a blend of older styles that made it look like something out of a fairy tale. Every room contained murals depicting figures from German legends, who were also the main characters in Wagner's operas.

The Singers' Hall at the top of the castle came from a scene in *Parsifal.* It had arched windows, a red-and-gold ceiling, and carved figures of angels and dragons holding up the beams. Gold chandeliers and enormous candelabra held 549 candles that were lit every evening. King Ludwig II kept odd hours—he stayed up all night and went to sleep at dawn. His blue-and-gold bedroom featured a magnificent four-poster bed carved as intricately as a Gothic cathedral. The canopy over the bed and the coverlet and

Singer's Hall, decorated
with scenes from
Wagner's opera *Parsifal*

draperies were made of heavy silk embroidered with little swans
wearing golden crowns. The adjoining bathroom was hung with
artificial stalactites so that he could feel as though he were bathing
in a cave.

The Throne Room was two stories high but held no throne at all.
Marble stairs led up to a golden alcove where the throne should
have been. In most castles throne rooms were used as places where
kings and queens received members of their court and important
visitors. Ludwig used his throne room as a place to meditate. The
domed ceiling was painted blue, his favorite color, and patterned
with golden stars. The floor was covered with mosaics picturing
animals and trees. It is said that the room, designed by Ludwig

himself, was intended to show that he, the king, stood between heaven and earth.

King Ludwig II supervised construction of the castle. From his family's old castle down below he looked through a telescope to check on the progress of his workers. A team of architects, masons, painters, sculptors, and decorators rushed to complete Neuschwanstein by Christmas of 1871. Architect Riedel was succeeded by Georg Dollmann, who, in turn, was replaced by Julius Hoffman. The crew included Dr. Hyazinth Holland who had taught history, literature, and fine art at a girls' school in Munich. Dr. Holland gave advice about the historical accuracy of the decorations. Secretly, Dr. Holland thought King Ludwig II was crazy. He wrote in his autobiography that Ludwig kept demanding bizarre changes such as a waterfall tumbling down one of the staircases. Fortunately, architect Dollmann talked him out of it.

The castle, still under construction in 1875

"Mad" King Ludwig II of Bavaria

Although Neuschwanstein looked medieval, in some ways it was up-to-date. Unlike most chilly castles, it had central heating. And in the kitchen there were underground ducts that carried away smoke from the chimney. Ludwig was so busy designing his castle that he hardly paid any attention to the Franco-Prussian War of 1870. At that time Germany was divided into many individual countries, including Bavaria and Prussia. Together they fought against France and won in 1871. But Ludwig didn't bother to attend victory celebrations.

Neuschwanstein wasn't ready until 1884. After the king moved in, he still wanted to make additions. Creating castles was his passion, and he expected his country to pay for his projects—Neuschwanstein, his favorite castle, and two others, Linderhof and Herrenchiemsee. If his cabinet ministers refused to give him the money, he had them dismissed and appointed new ones. Sometimes he chose ministers simply from their photographs. Once he sent a message to be delivered to the president of Parliament. It read: "Tell him I need several extra millions; the buildings are the necessary happiness of my existence."

Because building castles cost so much, he needed to obtain loans. So he ordered his aides to borrow money from the king of Sweden, the sultan of Turkey, and the shah of Iran. When this plan failed, he told his servants to go to Frankfurt and rob the Rothschild

Bank. The men traveled to Frankfurt but didn't go through with the robbery. They made up some excuse when they returned.

In May 1886, the situation reached a crisis. The rich people who had loaned money to King Ludwig warned him to pay his debts or else they would take over his castles. Companies supplying Neuschwanstein with gas and water also demanded payment for their unpaid bills and threatened the king with a lawsuit. Ludwig, in turn, proclaimed that he would kill himself or leave Bavaria. By this time the people of Bavaria, especially those opposed to a monarchy, had had enough.

Ludwig withdrew to Neuschwanstein and never appeared in public again. Rumors circulated that he was mad. It was said that he had invited his favorite gray horse to have dinner with him and instructed his servants to serve the food on the best china. Afterward the horse smashed the dishes.

Finally, the minister-president and the leading members of government met in Munich and plotted to get rid of King Ludwig II. They consulted with Dr. Bernhard von Gudden, a professor of psychiatry who declared him insane and therefore legally unfit to rule. It was decided that the king's uncle, Prince Luitpold, would take over as regent. A commission went to seize the king at Neuschwanstein and remove him from power. Ludwig ran to the top tower and almost jumped off. But Dr. von Gudden managed to take him away in a locked carriage and drove him to the small castle on Lake Starnberg.

On June 13, 1886, the day after they arrived, Ludwig asked permission to go for a walk along the lake with Dr. von Gudden. A few hours later the bodies of both men were found floating in the lake in less than 4 feet of water. No one knows what actually happened. Was King Ludwig murdered? Or did he suffer a heart attack? What happened to Dr. von Gudden?

King Ludwig had given orders for Neuschwanstein and his other two castles to be blown up after his death to keep them safe from an "uncultured world" that couldn't appreciate art. However, his wishes were ignored. Just one month after he died, Neuschwanstein was opened to the public, and it became Bavaria's most visited historical monument. Today it is Germany's most popular castle. Pictures of the castle appear on the covers of numerous guidebooks, for it has come to symbolize Germany. Author Christopher McIntosh praised Neuschwanstein for its "genuine originality." The narrator of a travel video about Bavaria called it "crazy but elegant," a "unique architectural gem."

If "imitation is the sincerest form of flattery," as poet Charles Caleb Colton wrote in the 1820s, the greatest tribute to the castle came from Walt Disney. In 1954, he built a replica of Neuschwanstein at Disneyland Park in Anaheim, California, and called it Sleeping Beauty Castle. He intended it as "a storybook castle." Disney wanted his theme park to convey a sense of magic, so he formed a castle as its centerpiece.

Artist Herbert Dickens Ryman drew the first rendering over a weekend. When the castle was constructed, it stood only 75 feet high.

Tricks of perspective were used to make it seem taller. The fake stones made of stucco varied in size. Bigger ones were placed at the bottom, with progressively smaller ones toward the top, making the castle appear to soar.

When Disneyland Park opened in July 1955, Walt Disney dedicated Fantasyland at the entrance to the Sleeping Beauty Castle. He had created a land "where dreams come true," just as King Ludwig II had realized *his* fantasy by building Neuschwanstein.

**Sleeping Beauty Castle in Disneyland's Fantasyland**

# CHAPTER SEVEN

# Solomon R. Guggenheim Museum,

## New York, New York

SOLOMON R. GUGGENHEIM, an eighty-two-year-old multimillionaire, had a problem. He loved art and had been collecting modern paintings and sculptures for years. His art was in a rented gallery in New York City, but by 1943 his collection had grown so large that he needed a bigger, permanent place. He also wanted to share it with the public. So he decided to build a museum. The curator who took care of Guggenheim's art, Baroness Hilla von Rebay, recommended Frank Lloyd Wright as the perfect architect for the job. In 1943 she sent a letter to Wright at Taliesin, his home and studio in Spring Green, Wisconsin, to see if he was interested.

Although Wright was considered a genius by some, he may have seemed a strange choice. For one thing, he hated cities, particularly New York, which he called "a forest of skyscrapers." And for another, he didn't like painting and thought it was inferior to architecture, which he considered to be "the mother art of arts." But the commission intrigued him. At that time Wright was seventy-six. Despite his long career spanning fifty years, he had never designed a museum before and had never done a major building in New York City, which he recognized as a cultural center.

Wright went to New York and met with von Rebay and Guggenheim to see the collection. He especially admired the abstract paintings of Wassily Kandinsky, the father of nonobjective art—art composed of colors and forms that didn't represent anything found in the real world. Wright and Guggenheim signed a contract two weeks after their meeting, and began to look for an appropriate site.

Back at Taliesin, Wright started to draw sketches of the proposed museum. At first he thought the structure should be low and horizontal like his Prairie Houses in the Midwest. But land in Manhattan was too expensive to hold a big horizontal building. So Wright experimented with a vertical form. During this period he had become interested in circular shapes. Geometry as well as nature had always influenced his work. The very first sketch for the museum showed intersecting circles drawn with a compass. Then he came up with a spiral shape topped by a dome. Wright wrote the word *ziggurat,* a Mesopotamian word meaning "to build high," on his drawing. He was referring to the ancient temples of Sumer, Assyria, and Babylon that were approached by ramps and grew smaller toward the top. But his design showed a spiral that grew larger as it rose.

Von Rebay loved the design. Guggenheim approved it and told Wright to go ahead with detailed plans. By spring 1944, the site had been chosen—an empty lot on Fifth Avenue facing Central Park between Eighty-eighth and Eighty-ninth Streets. This neighborhood was and still is one of the most desirable residential areas in New York City. Turn-of-the-century mansions and elegant limestone apartment buildings staffed by uniformed doormen lined the blocks around the museum's site. A narrow town house bordered the property on Eighty-eighth Street.

Wright's spiral design looked totally different from these traditional buildings. He saw the museum as "a little temple in the park," but when the drawings were first published, others called it everything from an "inverted potty" to a "gigantic snail shell." Wright *was* inspired by seashells, in particular "the spiraled perfection of the chambered nautilus."

He conceived of the museum as an airy, open place where visitors would not have to retrace their steps through small stuffy rooms. For the interior, he planned a continuous ramp curling around a great central space from the ground floor up to the sixth.

Wright compared it to an unbroken ocean wave. "A museum should be one extended expansive well-proportioned floor space from bottom to top," he said.

The space would be crowned by a domelike glass roof to provide natural light. Below the roof there would be a continuous band of skylights.

He worked out his ideas in a three-dimensional model. Guggenheim and von Rebay liked it and gave their approval. It was 1945, and World War II had just ended. Wright wanted to begin construction immediately, but Guggenheim predicted that building costs would soon come down. He thought that the museum could be constructed for less money if they waited a year. The project was put on hold. Rumors spread that perhaps the museum would never be built.

In 1946, Guggenheim bought the town house that stood alongside the site to use as a temporary home for his collection.

Frank Lloyd Wright, Baroness Hilla von Rebay, and Solomon R. Guggenheim with Wright's model

Wright advised Guggenheim not to waste money on this building because it would eventually be torn down when construction started. Instead, he suggested an eleven-story annex that would hold offices and additional galleries. Guggenheim agreed. Wright quickly produced working drawings and sent them to New York.

But Guggenheim became ill and died in November 1949 before the project was started. In his will, however, he stipulated that the museum be built and set aside money for it. The exact arrangements were left open-ended. Von Rebay bickered with Wright about the remaining details of the design of the museum. For example, he wanted the walls to be tilted like easels to show the paintings as the artists had seen them while they painted. She wanted alcoves or bays with straight-sided walls. Von Rebay accused Wright of planning the museum as a monument to himself. She feared that his innovative architecture would overpower the paintings, and her fears later proved to be true.

Another obstacle arose in 1950 when the Fifth Avenue Association objected to the building of the museum even though they had never seen plans or models. The association, formed in 1907, consisted of people who owned shops, hotels, and apartment buildings along stylish Fifth Avenue. They felt that the proposed modern museum would be out of character with their elegant neighborhood. Although they couldn't actually stop construction, they influenced the people in power.

So when Wright applied for a permit to the New York Building Department, he was turned down. The department said that the proposed museum didn't meet the city's building codes. They objected to poured concrete as a building material, clear glass in the doorways, the slope of the ramps, and the fact that the building at its highest point would bulge over Fifth Avenue. What's more, they said, the museum would be a potential firetrap.

At first Wright refused to make any changes. Eventually, though, he went back to the drawing board and revised his plans.

He appealed to the Building Department, and he also submitted his plans to Robert Moses, the powerful New York parks commissioner. Moses spoke up on Wright's behalf and said to the head of the city's Board of Standards and Appeals, "Damn it, get a permit for Frank. I don't care how many laws you have to break. I want the Guggenheim built." Finally the city officials gave Wright a building permit.

But 1953 brought new problems. Von Rebay resigned as curator of the museum and was replaced by James Johnson Sweeney. Sweeney and Wright clashed in nearly all their views. Sweeney thought Wright's design was too extreme and wanted Wright to tone it down. They disagreed about many details. Sweeney wanted stark white walls, while Wright wanted softer shades of cream and pink. Wright insisted on natural light, while Sweeney preferred fluorescent lights.

Construction was about to get underway, yet they had not worked out their differences. The Euclid Construction Company was chosen to build the museum. Wright rented an apartment in the Plaza Hotel in New York so that he could be on hand to closely supervise and make certain *his* plan was followed.

At last, on August 16, 1956, ground was broken and the site prepared. By this time Wright was eighty-nine years old but as feisty as ever. He appeared on the site, nattily dressed in his custom-made overcoat and porkpie hat. Gesturing with his cane, he pointed to sections that had to be changed.

As the museum went up, enclosed by scaffolding, New Yorkers were terribly curious. "Sidewalk superintendents" walked by and offered their comments. Newspapers and magazines published some of Wright's drawings and described his plans. The *New Yorker* magazine did a piece about the museum and asked the construction workers for their opinions. One worker thought the project was "screwy." "The whole joint goes round and round," he said.

"WHAT IS IT?" read a headline in another magazine article about the museum. Critics compared Wright's spiral-shaped building to a popover, a marshmallow, an oversize concrete mushroom, a giant corkscrew, an upside-down washing machine, and a Martian spaceship. *The New York Times* showed a photo of it with the

59

*"Are they allowed to do that on Fifth Avenue?"*

caption, "Hangar for Flying Saucers?"

Many New Yorkers believed that Wright was thumbing his nose at the city by building the Guggenheim Museum. Architectural historian Herbert Muschamps said the museum was "Wright's joke on New York."

"It is a freak that astonishes passersby," wrote journalist Brendan Gill. "It bears no relationship to its neighbors."

More complaints came from a group of New York artists whose work was going to be shown in the museum. On December 21, 1956, twenty-one painters including Milton Avery, Willem de Kooning, and Franz Kline sent a letter to the trustees of the museum protesting Wright's design. They felt that their pictures wouldn't hang right because of the spiraling ramp and sloping walls. "The interior design of the building is not suitable for a sympathetic display of painting and sculpture," they wrote.

Wright replied that they were wrong, and would paint better pictures under the influence of his gallery. He reminded them that Solomon Guggenheim had wanted something new and different and "not just another museum."

Despite the painters' protest, the building went on as planned. But Wright and Sweeney continued to argue about the color of the walls and how the paintings should be lit. Wright visited the site for the last time in January 1959, and gave instructions about the final touches. Then in the spring he suffered a series of dizzy spells. Wright went to the hospital for an operation and died on April 9, just before his ninety-second birthday.

**Wright on site**

When the museum officially opened on October 21, 1959, thousands of viewers stood in line, waiting to pay fifty cents admission. They came to see paintings by Wassily Kandinsky, Paul Klee, Pablo Picasso, Jackson Pollack, and some of the twenty-one artists who had signed the petition. But they paid more attention to the building. In the gift shop, postcards picturing the museum far outsold those showing the paintings exhibited.

Opinions about the new museum ranged from complaints about lack of storage space and seating to problems with the tilt of the ramp. Viewers felt off balance as they stood on an incline while looking at pictures hung on sloped walls. "Dizziness and even seasickness has reputedly replaced sore feet as the principal museum goer's disease at the Guggenheim," declared the Washington, D.C. *Sunday Star.* Muschamps complained that the ramp would be "more appropriate in a parking garage than in a

The museum's spiraling ramp and sloping walls

museum." But museum guards reported that most visitors enjoyed taking the elevator up to the sixth floor, then strolling down the ramp. Some were tempted to roller skate! Many newspapers and magazines printed rave reviews of the dramatic interior.

In the years following the opening, the Guggenheim Museum proved to be one of New York's most popular museums. The stretch of upper Fifth Avenue formerly called Millionaire's Row became known as Museum Mile. But a fresh controversy arose in 1992 when an addition to the Guggenheim designed by Charles Gwathmey and Robert Siegel went up. The new tower on Eighty-ninth Street provided much needed office and exhibition space. But people in the neighborhood complained that the tower cut off their light, fresh air, and view of Central Park. Some said that the Guggenheim with its addition now looked like a toilet bowl and tank. Although the tower was based on Wright's original design for an eleven-story annex, his loyal fans opposed changes made by other architects.

To this day the Guggenheim stirs up debate. Is it an art museum or a monument to the man who designed it? Is it a memorial to Frank Lloyd Wright or to Solomon R. Guggenheim?

"THE STRANGEST BUILDING OF THE YEAR."

"AN ARCHITECTURAL KING KONG."

"THE BACK OF A REFRIGERATOR, ENORMOUSLY ENLARGED."

# CHAPTER EIGHT

# Pompidou Center,
## Paris, France

ARCHITECTS RICHARD ROGERS and Renzo Piano of London, England, and Genoa, Italy, won an international competition held in 1971 to build a new cultural center in Paris. Up till then the young unknown architects had designed only some modest houses, two high-tech factories, a shopping center, and a prefab hospital. Excitedly, they flew to Paris in July for the reception. But at a televised press conference in a crowded auditorium, people in the audience attacked their design. The French were furious that two "foreigners," an Englishman and an Italian, had won. What's more, no one knew who the architects were. They had heard of the Danish engineers on their design team, Ove Arup and Partners, but who on earth were these brazen upstarts? One woman became so violent in her remarks that she had to be removed from the auditorium by the police.

The next morning, Rogers and Piano, dressed in blue jeans, along with other members of their team, went to the Elysée Palace and met President Georges Pompidou. Although Pompidou admired their design, he predicted that it would stir up controversy. *"Ça va faire crier*—that's going to cause an outcry," he said to his wife. However, Pompidou gave a little speech about the honor of working for Paris, the greatest city, and for France, the most cultured and enchanting country. Then he asked if there were any questions. The architects were tempted to inquire when they would receive their prize money so that they could afford to pay their hotel bill. Instead, Rogers requested the president's autograph for his children.

Rogers and Piano's model and drawings were exhibited in the Grand Palais along with all 681 entries. The other more traditional designs included pyramids, temples, supermarkets, and office buildings. A Russian team created a structure shaped like a gigantic hen to symbolize Culture laying golden eggs.

By comparison, Rogers and Piano's idea was simple, though bold and radical. "It does not look like anything one has ever seen before," wrote a critic. The scale model and drawings represented a high-tech structure that would be made of glass and steel. All of its mechanics such as water pipes, air ducts, and electrical wiring hung on the outside instead of being hidden behind walls and above ceilings. The point was to open up inside space. Even the elevators and escalators were pushed outside. It was described as "a building turned inside out."

Rogers and Piano envisioned a flexible structure that could easily be changed. Parts could be added, updated, and replaced.

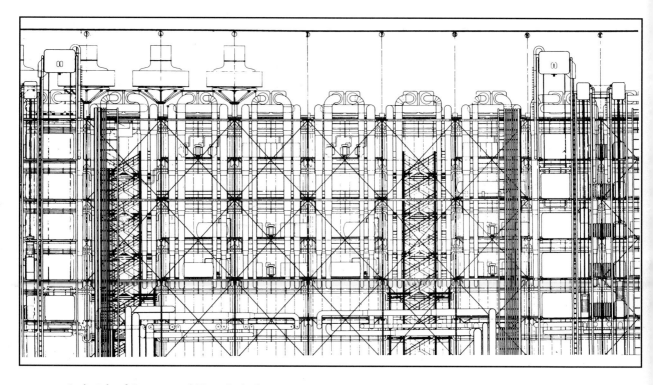

**A sketch of Rogers and Piano's design**

The pieces would fit together like pieces in a Lego set. Critics commented that the model looked as though it had been constructed from a toy kit. All of the elements were color coded. White was for the structure: columns, girders, and beams. Blue was for air-conditioning ducts, green for water pipes, and yellow for electrical wiring. Escalators, elevators, and fire apparatus were red.

The purpose of the new center was to provide the first major free public library in Paris, a modern art museum, an industrial design center, galleries for rotating exhibitions, and an institute for musical research. The center would also contain lecture halls, a movie theater, a restaurant, and bookshops. Since Rogers and Piano wanted it to be easy for people to go in and out, the model featured eleven entrances on all four sides rather than one main entrance. They hoped that neighborhood shoppers would take shortcuts through the building and enjoy seeing exhibits along the way.

Rogers and Piano planned an open space in front of the cultural center. "The centre is a public event," they wrote in the text accompanying their model and drawings. Their idea was to revive the ancient Paris tradition of street theater by providing a place for performers.

The site for the center was an old parking lot for trucks called Plateau Beaubourg on the right bank of the River Seine. It was at the edge of an historic district called the Marais that features some buildings that date back to medieval times. Crooked gabled buildings line the narrow streets. The oldest house in Paris, built in 1407, stands a block away from the center. None of the buildings was higher than three stories. So Rogers and Piano's proposed seven-story high-tech building did *not* blend in with the neighborhood. Pierre Schneider, a journalist reporting from Paris for *The New York Times,* described their project this way: "It is a glass-and-steel block dropped into the middle of a tortuous, still medieval quarter like a huge ice cube amidst crumbling pâté sandwiches."

It was said that winning an architectural contest in France did not guarantee that construction would take place, and the architects wondered if their building would ever get built. The deadline for completing the project was 1975. Optimistically, Rogers and Piano moved to Paris, found homes, opened offices, hired a staff, and began to work.

The first problem they faced was the language barrier. Of the team members, only Renzo Piano was fluent in French. Rogers had trouble just buying a pencil in Paris. However, the team communicated with their French coworkers by drawing. Traditionally French architects didn't participate in the actual construction of their projects, but Rogers and Piano did things their own way.

With the help of their head engineer, Ove Arup, they found a German manufacturer who could produce the unique prefabricated steel parts they needed. Everyone in the construction industry thought the design was ridiculous. When a French company, Grands Travaux de Marseilles (GTM), was finally chosen to do the building, the chief assistant kept putting down the structural design. "It will never work," he said.

Yet Rogers, Piano, and their team of architects and engineers forged on. Excavation began in 1972, but none of the details had been worked out for the concrete substructure. So Piano and Rogers had to develop their ideas as they went along. A major setback occurred in April 1974 when President Pompidou died. A new president, Valéry Giscard d'Estaing, took over along with a new political party and new cultural advisers. Why would they want to continue with an unpopular project named after their political rival? Rogers and Piano had to work hard to save the project.

As the frame of the structure went up and people saw what the center was going to look like, they objected even more furiously. Residents of Beaubourg brought "nuisance allegations" against the jury that had selected the winning design in the first place. A group of French architects formed an organization called the Geste Architecturale and filed lawsuits to stop the project. They succeeded in temporarily bringing it to a halt. Another group consisting of artists and leading intellectuals sent a petition to the director of Public Works. It said: "We writers, painters, sculptors, architects, all passionately concerned with that spirit of beauty

**The Center under construction**

which, till now, had been preserved intact in Paris, wish to protest with all possible strength, all possible indignation, in the name of French art and history, now menaced and threatened, against the erection, in the very heart of our capital, of this useless monster." The joke was that the petition had originally been drawn up one hundred years earlier in criticism of the Eiffel Tower.

Despite the protests, criticisms, and delays, the Pompidou Center was finally completed in December 1976. "NEW ARTS CENTER IN PARIS TO OPEN AMID RAGING CONTROVERSY" read the headline of an article written by Hilton Kramer in *The New York Times.* The article was illustrated with two cartoons drawn by artist Red Grooms. One showed the center standing out among other Paris landmarks with a caption calling it "an architectural King Kong." In the second cartoon a large woman symbolizing Paris tried on the Pompidou Center like a hat. The caption read: "La belle Paris has a new chapeau." At the end of the article, Kramer praised the building as "playful and even elegant."

When the Pompidou Center finally opened to the public in February 1977, journalists from all over the world had something to say. John Russell in *The New York Times* described it as "the new museum Parisians love to hate." English novelist Anthony Burgess called it "a $200 million Erector Set." The *Sunday Times* in Britain said it was "the strangest building of the year." British architectural historian Mark Girouard compared the side of the building on busy Rue de Renard to "the back of a refrigerator, enormously enlarged."

But Kramer said: "The astonishing building that houses the center is one of the most breathtaking architectural accomplishments of recent times, and certainly the most radical modernist building ever to be erected in Paris."

Visitors were shocked, baffled, and awed by the enormous pipes that looked like funnels on a ship painted in bright blue, green, yellow, and red. Some people thought that the scaffolding had been left up by mistake. Slowly they rode the escalators enclosed in glass tubes and marveled at the view of Beaubourg directly below them, and Paris beyond. Down in the square, clowns, acrobats, and fire-eaters entertained the public. In the fountain along the square, Jean Tinguely's colorful metallic sculptures shaped like giant lips and a fanciful elephant's head twirled, spun, and spouted water.

The Pompidou Center immediately attracted thousands of visitors. During the first year alone more people came to see it than visited the Eiffel Tower and the Louvre Museum combined. Quickly it became one of the most popular cultural sites in the world. At the end of 1977, art critic Ada Huxtable pronounced it "the Building of the Year."

Yet residents of the neighborhood had mixed opinions. Some still considered it a "cultural monster, in a place not really suited to it." Others worried that rents would be raised in apartments around the Pompidou Center. However, young people loved it because it stayed open, all lit up, till late at night and featured rock concerts as part of the cultural offerings. Students from every part of Paris used the vast library, video archive, and recording collection.

The escalators in glass tubes

From 1997 to 1999, the Pompidou Center closed for renovations under the supervision of the architects, Piano and Rogers. They were practicing separately but still good friends. Halfway through the job, though, Rogers left because he hated the changes so much. Not only did the center receive a fresh coat of paint, but the gallery spaces for showing art became smaller, and more enclosed and formal. After the center reopened in January 2000, visitors could no longer have a free ride up the outside escalator to enjoy the view. Now they have to buy tickets to the art museum up on the fourth and fifth floors. Architect Piano said, "I am unhappy about making people pay to go up the escalator, but these are inevitable things. Beaubourg isn't built for twenty years, but for three hundred, four hundred, five hundred years."

"IT'S LIKE A BUNKER."

"OUR AREA DESERVED BETTER."

"MORE LIKE A MINE SHAFT THAN A CIVIC BUILDING."

## CHAPTER NINE

# Walker Community Library,

## Minneapolis, Minnesota

WHY DID EVERYONE HATE the new Walker Community Library in Minneapolis, Minnesota?

For one thing, it was underground.

"I don't like working underground," said librarian Gary Cooper. "I feel cut off from the world. It gets really stuffy. It's like a bunker." It had an "uninviting dungeon atmosphere," commented Harley and Kimberly Toberman in a letter to the editor of the *Hill & Lake Press.* "We thought our area deserved better."

For another thing, people thought the library was ugly. "One of Minneapolis's most despised public buildings," wrote local journalist David Anger. It looks "more like a mine shaft than a civic building." To some, the part that appeared above ground resembled a jail.

Everyone missed the old library building across the street. For years it had been one of the busiest branches of the Minneapolis library system. Built in 1910 by the Carnegie Foundation, it stood on Hennepin Avenue near Lake Street. Andrew Carnegie, a business tycoon, gave library buildings to more than a thousand communities in America and Canada in the early part of the twentieth century. Known as "the Patron Saint of Libraries," Carnegie wanted to educate immigrant workers and children and to provide them with a good place for reading and getting together. A Scottish immigrant himself, he had made a fortune in the steel industry, and felt obligated to do something for other struggling newcomers.

Like many of the Carnegie libraries, the one on Hennepin Avenue was patterned after Greek architecture. Steep steps led up to an entrance marked by limestone columns supporting a triangular pediment carved with the words "Minneapolis Public Library." The idea was that libraries were "heroic places" where people would climb up to acquire knowledge.

The Walker Community Library served the Uptown area near Lake Calhoun for seventy years. Gradually the neighborhood became a lively commercial center. Although there were still a couple of mansions near the lake, and apartment buildings, Hennepin Avenue held rows of shops, an indoor mall, restaurants, two movie theaters, and a bus station. The bus route ran past the library. Sometimes passengers hopped off and went into the library to borrow books. In the wintertime, when temperatures fell to well below freezing they often slipped inside to get warm.

By the late 1970s, the old library building was too small to serve so many people. It didn't have meeting rooms for groups. What's more, the old library needed expensive improvements, such as rewiring to accommodate modern computers and access for people with physical handicaps.

At that time, during the late 1970s, the United States experienced an energy crisis. People worried about conserving natural resources.

So when architect David Bennett was hired to design a new library, he knew that building below street level would be more energy efficient. He estimated that the need for heating and cooling would be reduced by 40 percent. The land left on top could be used both for parking and as a little plaza for neighborhood events such as the annual art fair.

Most important, Bennett solved the problem of space. By going underground he could build a bigger library on a small site. Construction began in 1981. The library was made out of concrete and brick to blend in with the neighboring commercial buildings. Elevator and stairs at ground level led down to the "minus 1" level

**A window onto the sunken courtyard**

that contained meeting rooms. Below that, the "minus 2" level held the main library with books, magazines, and a circulation desk. Windows faced out to a sunken courtyard garden. Bennett knew that people needed to see the outdoors. Going underground made many people frightened because it reminded them of death and burial. Some felt trapped. So he designed higher than usual 20-foot ceilings to make the reading room seem airy. By sinking the reading room below street level, he shut out traffic noise and created a truly quiet place.

But people complained that the atmosphere was dark and gloomy. It reminded some of bomb shelters. The librarians joked about offering flashlights to patrons. Despite Bennett's efforts, a heading in the *Christian Science Monitor* described his structure as "a buried library."

A few critics liked it, though. The Walker Library had the distinction of being one of the first earth-sheltered buildings in the

United States. And Minneapolis architect Bernard Jacobs praised it for being "economical," a "novelty," and perhaps a "forerunner of similar" underground buildings. Others praised it as a "bold architectural statement."

But there were problems with the structure. The roof leaked. The heating system didn't work properly. Librarian Mary Ann Campbell grumbled that during the winter her nose was always cold. Patrons often wore parkas inside.

Outside, at street level, many people passed by without knowing that a library was there because it lacked a noticeable sign. The plaza area became a hangout for the homeless, skateboarders, and punk teenagers sporting wild hairdos. People threw trash from the street down into the garden.

Meanwhile, the underground library needed repairs. Harley and Kimberly Toberman came up with this suggestion: "Let's move everything back into the former building with a little tearoom downstairs. Then, convert the underground building into the new Hennepin County jail!"

Instead, the old library was sold. First it was used as a restaurant, then as a resale clothing store run by the Junior League.

In spring 1995 the Minneapolis Library Board hired architect Francis Bulbulian to remodel the underground library and make it work. First, Bulbulian fixed the leaks by simplifying the roof design. Then he reorganized the floor plan and enlarged the children's section. He moved it from the middle of the reading room to the end where it backed up against a curved wall. On the wall a mural based on a painting by Beatrix Potter showed Cinderella's coach drawn by bunnies and driven by mice. Carpeted steps with rounded corners led up to a mini-amphitheater for storytelling and puppet shows. Spotlights shone down on the stage.

The lighting inside the entire library was changed dramatically. Bulbulian cut two diamond-shaped windows in the concrete wall at the foot of the stairway. And he enlarged three windows facing the courtyard so that sunlight spilled into the reading area. "The dark, gloomy atmosphere has been driven out," wrote Peter

Millington in the *Lake Area News* when the library reopened on December 9, 1995.

Perhaps the architect's most innovative additions were 7-foot-high stainless steel letters on the plaza spelling L-I-B-R-A-R-Y. Now, no one could miss it! Kids loved to pose for photographs beside the first letter of their own name.

There was also a spiral metal book drop that Bulbulian made from a children's playground slide. He experimented by dropping a book down the slide and noticed that the spiral shape slowed down the book's descent. So he put two slides together, one on top of the other, to create something inexpensive that would work. "The book drop is definitely twenty-first century," wrote Millington. Kids wanted to slide down, and even adults were tempted to use it as an alternative entrance. Of course, the librarians wouldn't allow it. But they have been known to slide down the book drop into the library themselves from time to time.

After the library reopened, neighborhood groups finally had a place to get together. Groups such as Clutterers Anonymous, Overeaters Anonymous, the Girl Scouts, the Walker Book Club, and a writers' group called "the Loft" reserved the meeting rooms.

The plaza

**The book drop**

"Libraries—especially in the U.S.—have become much more than places to consult or borrow books," reported the magazine *World Architecture.* "They now serve as community centres, meeting social and cultural needs. Users are more likely to be socializing, eating, listening to music, or checking their e-mail, than reading a book." At the Walker branch, volunteer tutors help people work the computers. Kids from age eleven to fourteen sign up younger kids for the summer reading program. Bus drivers and their passengers still stop in to browse and borrow books. A large immigrant population of Asian, African, and Hispanic people come in to read books in their own languages as well as to learn English. Thus the new library serves the community in the very way that Andrew Carnegie originally intended. After the renovation, members of the neighborhood stopped griping and finally seemed to accept it, according to librarian Campbell.

Of course, there's still room for improvement. Campbell wishes they had a coffee shop like the Roseville Branch in Minneapolis. Many libraries now feature cafés and coffee bars to make the whole experience more enjoyable. The Central Library of the Los Angeles Public Library, for example, has a café that includes a fast-food restaurant and a place to buy frozen yogurt and desserts. Outside in the library garden there's an elegant white-tablecloth restaurant. These places were developed during the remodeling of the library, which added four underground levels lit by an arched skylight high overhead.

Many libraries go underground to use expensive city land efficiently and to save "green space"—precious grassy courtyards. The Doe Library at the University of California at Berkeley was rebuilt entirely underground. The Bowdoin College Library in Maine and the Carol A. Kroch Library at Cornell University in New York were also constructed underground. And the Redwood Library and Athenaeum in Newport, Rhode Island, one of the oldest libraries in the United States, will soon have an underground addition.

Elizabeth Downs-Reid, ten-year-old daughter of the Minneapolis district children's librarian, delighted in taking the elevator *down* to the main reading room. Proudly she said, "My mom's a librarian at the underground library."

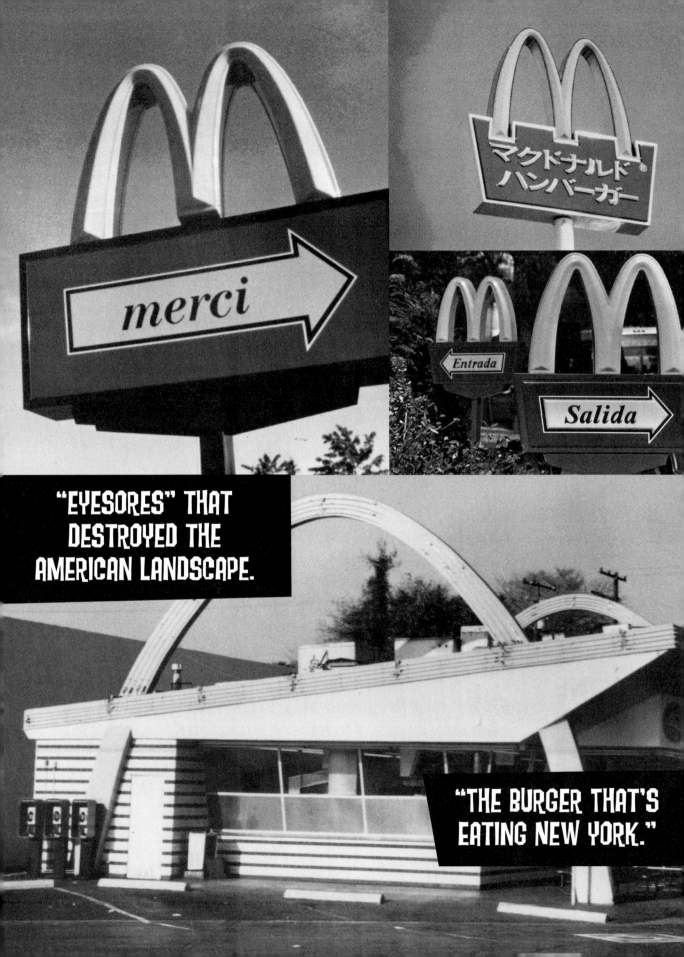

# CHAPTER TEN

# McDonald's,
## Worldwide

IN MILLAU, FRANCE, THE makers of goat cheese trashed the site of a new McDonald's while it was under construction. Meanwhile, farmers in another French town, Cavaillon, dumped rotten apples in the parking lot of their McDonald's. Why would adults do such a thing?

"We don't want one of these restaurants on every street corner in France," stated the leader of the cheese producers.

They resented American-style food taking over their town. There goes Millau, they thought. The Golden Arches have come to represent not only hamburgers and fries, but an American way of life. And the French prefer their own traditions. However, the McDonald's in Millau was built and ready for customers a month later, and the restaurant in Cavaillon reopened immediately.

There are hundreds of "McDos" in France, and thousands of McDonald's restaurants worldwide. A new McDonald's opens somewhere in the world every three hours.

But it all started back in 1952, with a single restaurant in San Bernardino, California. Richard (Dick) McDonald and his brother, Maurice (Mac), owned a drive-in called McDonald's that sold hamburgers for only fifteen cents, french fries for a dime, and milk shakes for twenty cents. With an emphasis on quick service, their sign showed a chubby little chef named Speedee.

The brothers prided themselves on cleanliness. Their octagonal building at Fourteenth and E Streets featured a spotless open kitchen in full view of the customers. They called it a "fishbowl" design. Kids loved getting a glimpse of a real restaurant kitchen. The self-service drive-in, the first of its kind, appealed to working-class families. For very little money they could all go out to dinner. The drive-in was so successful that other operators visited McDonald's, asked questions, took notes, and then copied the idea.

Dick and Mac wanted to branch out and build a chain of drive-ins. But they realized that they needed to make their building distinctive so that everyone would know at a glance that it was McDonald's and not some imitation. So they hired architect Stanley Meston of Fontana, California, to design a prototype, or experimental model.

Meston began by observing the store in San Bernardino and watching how the brothers turned out hamburgers and fries. "It was like designing a factory," he said. "There was a production line."

Of course, the restaurant had to be eye-catching for people driving by. Meston planned a rectangular place twice as big as the restaurant in San Bernardino, with stripes of red-and-white tiles on the outside, and a roof slanting down sharply from the front to the rear.

However, Dick wasn't entirely satisfied with the design. He thought the building looked too flat and needed some height. So one night he drew his own sketches. "I drew one big arch that ran parallel with the building, from side to side," he recalled, "and that looked kind of funny. So then I drew two arches running the other way." Meston developed the arches into elongated parabolic curves that in the 1950s expressed a futuristic look. When they were built, the arches stood 25 feet high. And the motif was repeated in a big sign out front.

Dick and Mac thought of painting the arches red, but instead chose yellow to contrast with the red-and-white tiles. Neon outlined the arches and trimmed the roof. At night the neon flashed on and off, attracting customers from blocks away.

"The whole thing was supposed to be a grabber," said Meston's assistant and chief draftsman. "The dramatic shapes and this big flaring roof and the high arches were something that would be immediately recognizable."

The first McDonald's with Golden Arches opened in May 1953 in Phoenix, Arizona. The next one went up in Downey, California. These McDonald's were franchised—that is, the brothers sold the

The Downey, California, McDonald's

rights to build and operate the restaurants to other people. But the new owners had to follow the design of the prototype and maintain the same menu and standards of cleanliness and service.

Around this time, Ray Kroc, a salesman who supplied restaurants with milk-shake machines, came out from Chicago to see the San Bernardino drive-in for himself. He couldn't understand why one little hamburger stand needed enough machines to make forty-eight milk shakes at the same time. He quickly realized why as he watched customers crowd the stand at lunchtime.

Right away, he saw a great opportunity. Most drive-ins were dingy and cheesy. But McDonald's was bright, clean, and offered good food at low prices. Kroc knew that the restaurants would appeal to young families. "He had seen cities all over the country, and he could just picture a McDonald's in every one of them," recalled a friend.

Kroc asked the McDonald brothers if he could be their franchising agent and sell their restaurants nationally. Dick and Mac didn't think the idea would work in colder climates. But they finally agreed, and in 1954 struck a deal.

Kroc formed a new company, McDonald's System, Inc., and built his showcase store in Des Plaines, Illinois. It opened in April 1955, and looked just like the McDonald's in Phoenix and Downey.

Under Kroc's leadership, the company grew rapidly. New restaurants opened in Illinois, California, Indiana, and Wisconsin. Signs outside soon announced: "WE HAVE SOLD OVER 1 MILLION HAMBURGERS," and the number kept going up daily. All employees including managers and cooks trained at Hamburger University in Elk Grove Village, Illinois. Real estate representatives flew around the country scouting for sites to build new McDonald's. "Look for schools, church steeples, and new houses," Kroc told them. He knew that children would be good customers because they liked ordering their own food, could afford fifteen-cent hamburgers, and enjoyed watching the cooking process. During the late 1950s and early 1960s, more than one thousand restaurants designed like the original Golden Arches were constructed throughout the United States.

But many people objected to having a garish hamburger stand in their neighborhood. The fast-food restaurants didn't blend in with residential areas. Neighbors complained about the unattractive backs of the restaurants. Zoning boards and local officials tried to prevent the structures from going up. In the Blue Mountains of Kentucky, for example, a group calling themselves "Mountains Against McDonald's" staged a campaign against the construction of a few Golden Arches.

Kroc toned down the arches by replacing the neon with fluorescent bulbs and yellow plastic covers. But architectural critics called the hamburger stands "eyesores" that destroyed the American landscape. In the 1960s, with a growing concern about the environment, public protest against McDonald's reached a new high. So the corporation hired architect Donald E. Miller to change the prototype. Miller lowered the arches, removed them from the roof, and later reduced them to a logo—a pair of linked arches shaped like the letter *M*. He also changed the roof design. Now it sloped in a mansard style, and he added wooden shingles to make it appear more homey. On the West Coast, types of building materials that fit in better with local buildings were used, such as adobe blocks and stone. Large patios planted with trees and shrubs provided pleasant outdoor eating areas. And indoors, more seating turned the drive-in into a real restaurant.

Dick Brams, head of advertising at McDonald's, thought up a way to win kids over. He packaged a hamburger, fries, and a soft drink in a box designed as a circus train and called it the "Happy Meal." Kids loved it and wanted to go to McDonald's more than ever. Paul Schrage, head of the marketing department, came up with another idea for making McDonald's attractive to families. In the 1970s he introduced playgrounds for kids that were just outside the restaurants. These areas featured Ronald McDonald and other McDonaldland characters—Mayor McCheese, Officer Big Mac, and the Grimace—as playground equipment. The "Playlands" had climbing towers, slides, and outdoor picnic tables colored in bright shades of red, yellow, blue, and green.

Yet some neighbors still protested violently when they heard that a new McDonald's was going up in their town.

The strongest protest occurred during the summer of 1974 in New York City. McDonald's planned to put up an office building with their restaurant on the main floor. The location was the corner of Lexington Avenue and Sixty-sixth Street, a fashionable residential area. Members of the neighborhood included bankers, society people, political figures, writers, and architects.

The "Friends of Sixty-sixth Street" collected the signatures of 1,500 neighbors on a petition. The "Friends" picketed the site and made the evening news on TV. Editorials in *The New York Times* denounced the proposed McDonald's, and the food editor of *The New York Times* magazine wrote an article about the fight in a cover story titled, "THE BURGER THAT'S EATING NEW YORK." For months McDonald's and the neighbors waged what came to be known as "the Battle of Lexington."

Finally, the protesters won. Although McDonald's built an office

Bordeaux, France

building on the site, they put a women's clothing boutique on the main floor instead of a fast-food restaurant.

Despite this one failure at home, McDonald's succeeded in expanding internationally. During the 1970s, they established fast-food restaurants around the world. Sometimes in addition to offering American food, they appealed to local tastes. For example, in Japan they served fried egg burgers called "moon-viewing burgers." And in India, where many people don't eat beef, the menu included Vegetable McNuggets and mutton burgers. But mostly they attempted to change local eating habits.

Once, in Germany, they tried to do this by making the interior of the restaurant look like a typical beer hall with dark colors, lots of wood, and dim lighting. They soon found out, however, that the stores did best when they looked like the standard American version, complete with Golden Arches.

The Golden Arches have become a symbol of American popular culture. Many Americans treasure the early McDonald's restaurants as "cultural artifacts." The hamburger stand in Downey, California, the oldest operating McDonald's on the planet, has been preserved by the town's historical society. Thanks to the effort of architect and critic Alan Hess, the stand qualified to be included in the National Register of Historic Places. And the McDonald's in Des Plaines, Illinois, has been rebuilt and kept as a museum.

So whether or not you like Big Macs and fries, the sight of a McDonald's surely reminds you of America—big, bright, and successful.

San Juan, Puerto Rico

# GLOSSARY

**annex**—an addition to a building

**architect**—a person who designs buildings

**bay window**—a window or series of windows that jut out of a wall and form a bay

**bungalow**—a one-story cottage

**colonial style**—houses similar in design to those built in the colonies at the time of the American Revolution

**foundation**—the base, usually underground, on which a building rests

**gable**—the end of a pitched roof formed by the sloping sides

**gallery**—an upper story of a building, such as a balcony, or a large room or building used for special purposes, such as art exhibits or parties

**girder**—a large beam made of wood, steel, or concrete, used for supporting masonry

**Gothic style**—an eighteenth-century revival style first made popular in England, inspired by churches built throughout Europe in the Middle Ages

**landscape architect**—a person who designs parks, gardens, or parkways

**masonry**—building materials such as stones, bricks, or cement

**mausoleum**—a small building that is a burial place for one person or members of one family

**obelisk**—a pillar with four sides that taper to a point

**pavilion**—a small open building usually found in a garden

**pediment**—a triangular space above a door or window

**podium**—in architecture, a massive platform on which an ancient building was sometimes placed

**prefab**—sections of a building constructed beforehand, then quickly assembled

**prototype**—the original model for something that will be built

**scale model**—a small version of a structure built in exact proportions to its full size

**skyscraper**—a tall building of many stories, supported by a metal frame, invented in the United States of America around the turn of the century

**spire**—a tall pointed end of a roof or tower

**stucco**—a material usually made of cement and sand, used for covering the exterior of a building

**terra-cotta**—a hard-fired clay, often brownish red, that is used for architectural ornaments

**turret**—a small tower that is part of a larger building, such as a castle or fortress

# NOTES ON SOME OF THE ARCHITECTS

### David Bennett (1935–)

David Bennett grew up in Brooklyn, New York, and studied sculpture at the Cooper Union for the Advancement of Science and Art in New York City. He earned his degree in architecture from the University of Minnesota. "I had the romantic notion that American architecture was born in the Middle West," he said, "and that's where I would find it."

From 1973 to 1994, Bennett was the founder and principal of BRW Architects, Inc., in Minneapolis. He pioneered underground architecture as a solution to the energy crisis. Bennett worked with engineers in creating his first underground building, Williamson Hall at the University of Minnesota in Minneapolis. To preserve as much open space as possible on this crowded campus, he placed 95 percent of the building beneath the earth's surface. Skylights tilted at an angle in office areas let in natural light and offered pleasing views of the courtyard. Williamson Hall, completed in 1977, won many prestigious awards.

One of his greatest successes was the Civil/Mineral Engineering Building (C/ME Building), completed in 1983 at the University of Minnesota. By using a system of lenses and mirrors that reflect the sun all day long, Bennett projected natural light down into this building, 110 feet below the earth's surface. A device like a periscope allowed people to get a view of the campus above. Bennett called his high-tech building "an earthship." The C/ME Building won state and national awards in architecture, engineering, and lighting design. Currently Bennett has a consulting firm, DJB Architects, and splits his time between Minnesota and New York.

### Daniel Hudson Burnham (1846–1912)

Daniel Hudson Burnham decided to become an architect when he was a young man. He worked for a firm helping to rebuild Chicago after the Great Fire had leveled the city. There he met architect John Wellborn Root and in 1873 formed a company with him.

Their first important job was to design a mansion for John B. Sherman, a stockyard tycoon. Sherman loved the house and his daughter, Margaret, loved Burnham. Burnham married Margaret and through her he met new society friends who became clients.

Burnham and Root collaborated on many of the most important buildings of their day, including one of the first skyscrapers, the ten-story Montauk Building, and the first modern office building, the exquisite "Rookery," where they had their own office.

In 1890, Burnham and Root headed a team to design buildings and grounds for the Chicago world's fair, known as the Columbian Exposition. However, Root died suddenly of pneumonia in 1891 at the age of forty-one, and Burnham had to carry on alone. The Exposition opened in May 1893 and drew thousands of visitors from all over the world. Burnham's showcase city, called the White City, served as a model for American architects and established his reputation as a city planner.

In 1901, President Theodore Roosevelt appointed Burnham head of a commission to redesign Washington, D.C. At that time railroad tracks crossed the Mall, and one of Burnham's ideas was to relocate the trains and build a station elsewhere. He realized his goal with the magnificent Union Station that is still in use today.

By 1912, Burnham's architectural company was one of the largest in the world and mainly designed skyscrapers. The triangular Fuller Building in New York is an elegant example of their work. The Field Museum of Natural History in Chicago was completed by Burnham's company after his death.

## Gustave Eiffel (1832–1923)

Gustave Eiffel grew up in Dijon, France. When he visited Paris for the first time with his father, he fell in love with the city and vowed to return. In 1850, Eiffel moved to Paris and attended the Polytechnic, a college. After graduating with a degree in chemical engineering, he worked as a secretary for a railway construction engineer.

Soon Eiffel designed his first metal structure, the Bordeaux Bridge across the Garonne River. It was a great success and led to his promotion. In 1866, he went into business for himself and constructed many metal bridges and viaducts throughout France, Europe, and the French colonies.

He built the iron frame for the Magasin au Bon Marché, the first modern glass-and-iron department store. It is still standing. Many people may not know that he worked on the Statue of Liberty. The sculptor, Auguste Bartholdi, hired Eiffel to design an iron framework to support the massive copper statue. However, Eiffel regarded the 1,000-foot tower in Paris as his greatest achievement.

"I ought to be jealous of the tower," he wrote in his memoirs toward the end of his life. "It is much more famous than I am."

He died a wealthy man and left the Eiffel Tower to his children and grandchildren as a family-run business called the Societé de la Tour Eiffel (S.T.E.), co-owned by shareholders. After Eiffel's death, the City of Paris did nothing special to honor him. But his landmark tower stands as a lasting tribute.

## Frank O. Gehry (1929–)

Frank O. Gehry's Guggenheim Museum in Bilbao, Spain, a branch of Frank Lloyd Wright's museum in New York City, has been hailed as one of the great architectural works of the twentieth century. When it opened in 1997, critics raved and tourists flocked to see it. The strange curving shapes covered in titanium have been compared to everything from a ship's sails to the petals of a flower unfolding to a silver mermaid. Some people say that the art museum looks like a piece of sculpture itself.

Gehry studied art before he took up architecture. Born in Toronto, Canada, he moved to Los Angeles when he was eighteen and received a degree in architecture from the University of Southern California. At Harvard University Graduate School of Design, Gehry studied city planning, but he dropped out and returned to California where he began working for architecture firms. In 1962, he established his own firm. With his wife, Berta, he bought and remodeled the little pink house in Santa Monica that created an uproar and won him fame. From that time on clients have come to him from all over the world.

Art critics have tried to give his style a name, but he says, "I'm a do what you feelist."

## Philip Johnson (1906–)

Philip Johnson is called the dean of American architecture and is probably one of the oldest practicing architects in the United States, if not the world. His office is in the Seagram Building on Park Avenue in New York City. Johnson designed this sleek steel, glass, and bronze skyscraper in 1958 with his mentor and associate, the great German-born architect Ludwig Mies van der Rohe.

Although he claims, "I'm not a big-name architect," Johnson has been a prominent figure in the profession since he began his career. After graduating from Harvard in 1930, he became the first director of the Department of Architecture and Design at the Museum of Modern Art in New York, and an important practitioner and champion of the International Style of architecture.

In 1942, Johnson returned to Harvard to study architecture and built a glass house for himself in Cambridge, Massachusetts. The house is still standing. Looking back, Johnson realized that he had made mistakes with that house. So he improved the design with the Glass House in New Canaan, Connecticut, in 1949.

During the course of his career Johnson has taught, lectured, written books, and designed many exciting landmark projects. In New York City alone he created the sculpture garden at the Museum of Modern Art, the New York State Theater and plaza at Lincoln Center, and two other skyscrapers—the AT&T Building and the "Lipstick" Building, so called because its rounded shape resembles a tube of lipstick. Wit and elegance characterize Johnson's beautiful buildings.

## Frederick Law Olmsted, Jr. (1870–1957)

Frederick Law Olmsted, Sr., known as the Father of American Landscape Architecture, was also the father of Frederick Law Olmsted, Jr., who was nicknamed Rick. Olmsted, Sr., combined his love of nature and his concern for society in designing open public places for people to enjoy, such as Central Park in New York City. He always hoped that his son would carry on his work.

Fulfilling his father's wishes, Olmsted, Jr., helped to establish the American Society of Landscape Architects in 1899, and taught the first courses in the subject at Harvard. In 1901, President Theodore Roosevelt assigned him to the Senate Park Commission to redesign the center of Washington, D.C. The commission was headed by Chicago architect Daniel Burnham. At that time the Mall was a messy pasture! Olmsted, Jr., suggested beautifying the grounds by planting rows of trees and creating playing fields and a system of connecting parks. However, the plan was not fully realized until 1929.

Over the years, Olmsted, Jr., received thousands of commissions for planning city, state, and national parks, college campuses, and residential communities.

### Renzo Piano (1937–)

Renzo Piano is not a musician but an architect. He grew up in Genoa, Italy, and studied architecture in Milan. At the time he met Richard Rogers he was working on projects in Osaka, Japan, and Harrisburg, Pennsylvania. Like Rogers, he was concerned with the needs of people who would use his buildings, and he favored high-tech, functional architecture. Piano considers himself an industrial designer as well as an architect. In 1970 he formed a partnership with Rogers and they maintained two offices—one in London and one in Genoa.

Today Piano has his own architectural firm in Genoa, where he redesigned the old docks and converted the harbor into a luxury port. Another commission was The Menil Collection of African and modern art in Houston, Texas.

In 1992, Piano designed the Kansai Air Terminal made of steel and glass in Osaka, Japan. One of its best features, though, is that it withstood the 1995 Kobe earthquake. He was awarded the Pritzker Architecture Prize in 1998. In 2000, his design for a new headquarters for *The New York Times* won an international competition.

### Richard Rogers (1933–)

Richard Rogers, now Lord Rogers, is an Englishman who comes from an Italian family. He met Italian architect Renzo Piano in 1968 or 1969 when a doctor friend introduced them.

Although the two are no longer partners, they are still friends. Rogers's office is located on a wharf at the River Thames in London. Clients come to him from all over the world.

Rogers views buildings not just as structures designed to please clients who pay for them, but also as part of the urban environment shared by everyone. The look of his architecture is high-tech. Prefab steel parts are set into place right on the site. In a bank building for Lloyd's of London, for instance, an entire stainless steel "toilet capsule," containing everything from sinks and stalls to lights and mirrors, was lowered into place by cranes. Among the many projects that Rogers and his teams of architects have designed and constructed are private houses throughout England, a laboratory in Princeton, New Jersey, an office building in Como, Italy, a restoration of the banks of the River Arno in Florence, Italy, and a factory in South Wales. What do all of these structures have in common? Steel parts painted in bright primary colors—yellow, red, blue, and green—just like the Pompidou Center.

### Frank Lloyd Wright (1867–1959)

"I was born an architect," boasted Frank Lloyd Wright. He was born in Richland Center, Wisconsin, and at the age of nineteen ran away to Chicago to learn just *how* to be an architect. One of his first jobs was with a firm headed by Dankmar

Adler and Louis Sullivan. Wright stayed with them for seven years before striking out on his own. After he married he designed a house for his bride in Oak Park, a suburb of Chicago, and later added a studio for his workplace and a vast, barrel-vaulted playroom for his six children. The house featured many original ideas such as low horizontal lines, prominent eaves that reflected the flat landscape. Wright's new style of architecture was called the Prairie School.

Wright's early houses impressed many leading Chicago architects, including Daniel Burnham. "Uncle Dan," as Wright called him, offered to send Wright to school in Paris to study classical architecture, with the promise of a job upon his return. But Wright refused because he wanted to retain his unique style.

As Wright's reputation grew, he received commissions for office buildings and churches as well as houses. Then in 1909, at the height of his career, he left his wife, children, and busy practice, and took off for Europe with the wife of one of his clients.

When he finally returned to the United States, he built a house in Spring Green, Wisconsin, and called it Taliesin. Many of his old clients disapproved of his behavior and dropped him, but a few loyal friends and admirers still gave him work. Some commissions took him out to California and as far away as Japan. In 1932, during the hard years of the Great Depression, Wright established the Taliesin Fellowship, an unusual school for apprentices who learned by working with him on his projects. With the help of his apprentices, Wright produced masterpieces such as Fallingwater, a house built over a waterfall in Bear Run, Pennsylvania, and the Johnson Wax Company administration building in Racine, Wisconsin. One of his last and most controversial projects was the Solomon R. Guggenheim Museum in New York.

# SELECTED BIBLIOGRAPHY

**Books**

Diamonstein, Barbaralee. *The Landmarks of New York III.* New York: Harry N. Abrams, Inc., 1998.

Dunlop, Beth. *Building a Dream: The Art of Disney Architecture.* Illustrated by Vincent Scully. New York: Harry N. Abrams, Inc., 1996.

Dupré, Judith. *Skyscrapers.* New York: Black Dog & Leventhal Publishers, Inc., 1996.

Freidel, Frank, and Lonnelle Aikman. *George Washington: Man and Monument.* Washington, D.C.: Washington National Monument Association, 1965.

Greenberg, Jan, and Sandra Jordan. *Frank O. Gehry: Outside In.* New York: Dorling Kindersley Publishing, Inc., 2000.

Hess, Alan. *Googie: Fifties Coffee Shop Architecture.* San Francisco: Chronicle Books, 1985.

Kreitler, Peter Gwillim. *Flatiron: A Photographic History of the World's First Steel Frame Skyscraper, 1901–1990.* Washington, D.C.: The American Institute of Architects Press.

Lynch, Anne, ed. *Great Buildings.* Alexandria, VA: Time-Life Books, 1996.

Macaulay, David. *Castle.* Boston: Houghton Mifflin Company, 1977.

———. *Building Big.* New York: Houghton Mifflin Company, 2000.

Murphy, Jim. *The Great Fire.* New York: Scholastic Inc., 1995.

Polley, Jane, ed. *Stories Behind Everyday Things.* Pleasantville, New York: Reader's Digest Association, 1980.

Rubin, Susan Goldman. *Frank Lloyd Wright.* New York: Harry N. Abrams, Inc., 1994.

Tompkins, Peter. *The Magic of Obelisks.* New York: Harper & Row, 1981.

Wilkinson, Philip. *Amazing Buildings.* Illustrated by Paolo Donati. New York: Dorling Kindersley, Inc., 1993.


**Videocassettes**

*Imperial Splendors.* Produced and directed by James Money-Kyrle. 58 min. IVN Communications/Reader's Digest Video and Television, 1996.

*Philip Johnson: Diary of an Eccentric Architect.* Produced and directed by Barbara Wolf. 55 min. Checkerboard Productions, 1996.

*Travel the World/Germany: Munich and Bavaria, Berlin and Potsdam.* Produced by John Givens. 53 min. Small World Productions/Oregon Public Broadcasting/American Program Service, 1995.


**Interviews**

Philip Johnson, architect, interview by author, at the Glass House, October 14, 1997.

Philip Johnson, architect, interview by author, at the Seagram Building, June 2, 1999.

Keith Mendenhall, assistant to Frank O. Gehry, interview by author, at Frank Gehry's house, April 28, 1999.

Jonathan W. Drezner, architect, interview by author, at Frank Gehry's house, April 28, 1999.

Mary Ann Campbell, librarian, interview by author, at the Walker Community Library, October 20, 1997.

David Bennett, F.A.I.A. telephone interview with author, August 9, 2000.

Charles W. Fish, A.I.A. emeritus, telephone interview with author, July 14, 2000.


**Web sites**

www.mcdonalds.com

www.centrepompidou.fr

www.nthp.org for the National Trust for Historic Preservation

www.nps.gov/wamo/monument/monument.htm (National Mall) for the Washington Monument

www.tour-eiffel.fr for the Eiffel Tower

www.schlossneuschwanstein.de for Neuschwanstein

# WHERE TO FIND OUT MORE ABOUT ARCHITECTURE:

Canadian Centre for Architecture
1920 Baile Street
Montreal, Quebec
Canada H3H 2S6
(514) 939-7026
www.cca.qc.ca/

Chicago Architecture Foundation
Administrative Offices
224 South Michigan Avenue
Chicago, IL 60604-2505
www.architecture.org/

Chicago Historical Society
Clark Street at North Avenue
Chicago, IL 60614-6099
(312) 642-4600
www.chicagohs.org/chshome.html

Cooper-Hewitt National Design Museum
Smithsonian Institution
2 East 91 Street
New York, NY 10128
(212) 849-8400
www.si.edu/ndm/

Frank Lloyd Wright Home and Studio
   Foundation
951 Chicago Avenue
Oak Park, IL 60302
(708) 848-1976
www.wrightplus.org

The Great Buildings Collection
www.greatbuildings.com

Landmarks Preservation Commission of
   New York City
100 Old Slip
New York, NY 10005
(212) 487-6800
www.ci.nyc.ny.us/html/lpc/home.html

The Museum of Modern Art
11 West 53 Street
New York, NY 10019
(212) 708-9400
www.moma.org

The National Building Museum
401 F Street NW
Washington, DC 20001
(202) 272-2448
www.nbm.org

National Registry for Historic Places
National Park Service
1849 C Street NW
NC400
Washington, DC 20240
(202) 343-9536
www.nps.gov/

New-York Historical Society
2 West 77 Street
New York, NY 10024
(212) 873-3400
www.nyhistory.org/

The Skyscraper Museum
First Place and Battery Place
New York, NY 10006
www.skyscraper.org/

Solomon R. Guggenheim Museum
1071 Fifth Avenue
New York, NY 10128-0112
(212) 423-3500
www.guggenheim.org/new_york_index.html

# INDEX

Page numbers in italic type refer to photographs and illustrations.